The Faithful
DOG

The Faithful
DOG

Contributing Editor
FERN COLLINS

CHARTWELL
BOOKS

Quarto is the authority on a wide range of topics.

Quarto educates, entertains and enriches the lives of our readers—enthusiasts and lovers of hands-on living.

www.quartoknows.com

This edition published in 2016 by
CHARTWELL BOOKS
an imprint of Book Sales
a division of Quarto Publishing Group USA Inc.
142 West 36th Street, 4th Floor
New York, NY 10018
USA

ISBN-13: 978-0-7858-3477-9

10 9 8 7 6 5 4 3 2 1

Printed in China

For all editorial enquiries, please contact:
www.regencyhousepublishing.com

Images used under license from
©Shutterstock.com

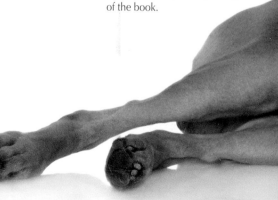

Flush or Faunus

Elizabeth Barrett Browning (1806–1861)

You see this dog. It was but yesterday
I mused, forgetful of his presence here,
Till thought on thought drew downward tear on tear;
When from the pillow, where wet-cheeked I lay,
A head as hairy as Faunus, thrust its way
Right sudden against my face,—two golden-clear
Large eyes astonished mine,—a drooping ear
Did flap me on either cheek, to dry the spray!
I started first, as some Arcadian
Amazed by goatly god in twilight grove:
But as my bearded vision closelier ran
My tears off, I knew Flush, and rose above
Surprise and sadness; thanking the true Pan,
Who, by low creatures, leads to heights of love.

CONTENTS

INTRODUCTION

Throughout recorded history, mankind's enduring association with the dog has been well-documented in many ways – in sculpture, in art, on film, and in literature. Art from the Babylonian Empire over 5,000 years ago clearly depicts huge, mastiff-type dogs. There can be little doubt that these animals were valued comrades in battle and probably performed guard duties as well. Fleet-footed sighthounds like the Greyhound and the Pharaoh Hound feature as drawings on the walls of Egyptian tombs dating back to 4000BC, indicating clearly

Sighthounds remarkably like this Greyhound feature on the walls of ancient Egyptian tombs.

OPPOSITE: A statue of the Egyptian god Anubis represented as a dog-headed human.

not only the presence of such breeds at that time, but also their significance in the lives of the people in these ancient empires. Indeed, so important was the dog considered during this period that it was worshipped in the form of the god Anubis, which is represented as a dog-headed human.

In the Middle Ages, dogs were frequently depicted in scenes, and the Bayeux Tapestry clearly shows Bloodhound-type dogs riding into battle with the Norman army. Later, in the 18th and 19th centuries, for example, it often seems that scarcely a painting was commissioned without a dog appearing in it somewhere – sitting diligently at its owner's feet, lying resplendent by the fire, or joining the hunters with their guns. Van Eyck, Gainsborough, Hogarth, and Landseer were among the many famous artists whose work has helped to immortalize dogs in art.

More recently, dogs have featured in literature. No one who has ever read Dodie Smith's book

The Hundred and One Dalmatians, or watched the film, will ever forget those endearing dogs and their antics as they try to escape from being made into an overcoat by the villainous Cruella De Vil. Then there is Buck, the half St Bernard and half shepherd dog that is the hero of Jack London's bittersweet epic tale *A Call of the Wild*.

Although many dogs make delightful pets, the huge range of breeds seen today has not come about because humans wanted a bigger choice of house companions! It is because most breeds of dog were designed to perform a particular duty – the fact that many of these breeds also have a friendly nature and adapt well to living in our houses as pets is something of a bonus. Although the need for dogs to carry out certain types of work has diminished, in other working situations they are as valued and important as ever they were.

No one has yet discovered a better all-round detector of drugs or explosives than the canine nose. The police forces of the world would probably rather have

OPPOSITE: The Newfoundland was immortalized by Sir Edwin Henry Landseer RA (1802- 1873) in his painting *Lion: A Newfoundland Dog*, 1824.

The Dalmatian was made famous in Dodie Smith's *The Hundred and One Dalmatians*.

a well-trained German Shepherd Dog by their side when dealing with a rowdy gathering than any other sort of deterrent. Rounding up a flock of hillside sheep without a dog such as a Collie would be an almost impossible task. Many blind people would face an isolated and lonely future without the intelligent seeing eyes of a kindly Labrador to help them. The list is endless.

Today, interest in dogs and all things canine is as great as it has ever been. As we find ourselves increasingly under pressure at work or because of the tensions in the world, so the simpler things in life – like a relaxing country ramble with a dog – take on a greater significance. Dogs fulfill a need in a way that no other animal can; we need them and we feel gratified that they seem to need us, too. For people living alone, a dog is a perfect companion, and for a growing family a dog is the instant playmate that expects to join in every bit of fun.

A well-trained and happy dog makes a loving friend; it is always willing to participate in whatever you want to do, it won't criticize, it won't sulk for too long if it can't get its own way, it guards the house and alerts you to visitors, it gets you out and about, and each has its own unique character that can amuse for hours. The therapeutic value of dogs is welL-known, too, and their usefulness in reducing stress and encouraging calmness in people around them cannot be overemphasized. But for this happy coexistence to occur, it takes effort on both parts and a degree of dedication and a lot of common sense and patience from you. Inevitably, a huge industry has grown up to cater for our love of dogs. Unfortunately, this has not always worked to the advantage of dogs or

For centuries the Border Collie has been an important and loyal farmworker.

their owners. Unscrupulous breeders have sometimes offered poor-quality animals, particularly if the breed is popular and in demand. This practice reduces the quality of the breed overall – especially if such animals are then bred on – and may even result in dogs with behavioral problems. Happily, it should be possible to avoid difficulties like this by buying a pedigree dog only from a reputable breeder. On the positive side, there has never been more choice of potential canine pets or working companions available to the would-be buyer. Once purchased, every aspect of a dog's nutrition, entertainment and general well-being can easily be provided for – there are even companies specializing in offering holiday accommodation designed to give a welcome to our dogs, too!

The descriptions found later in this book cover over 100 of the most popular breeds from all over the world. They will hopefully provide an insight into the varied and fascinating world of dogs.

Dogs make wonderful pets for people of all ages.

THE HOUND GROUP

The common feature of all the dogs in this group is that they pursue game. Being able to hunt out the quarry was a particularly important requisite before the advent of efficient guns.

Most of the dogs in this group are hounds that hunt by sniffing the ground to pick up and then follow a scent, calling and barking all the while. Dogs of this type include Beagles and Bassets.

Some hounds hunt primarily by sight. Among the best-known of the sighthounds is the Greyhound. Sighthounds rely on their eyes, rather than their noses, to detect prey before giving chase. Then, the dogs use their enormous speed and power to overtake and dispatch the quarry. In some Middle Eastern countries hunters on horseback take with them their sighthounds, which are released once a quarry is sighted. Other typical sighthounds include Salukis, Whippets and Afghan Hounds – all characterized by their long-legged, supple, and slender bodies capable of carrying the dog at speed.

There are some hounds that encompass both the virtues of the scenthounds and the sighthounds. They include the Pharaoh Hound and the Ibizan Hound, characterized by their sleek appearance and large, erect ears.

In addition to their skills as hunters and trackers, many hounds also make excellent guard dogs. Generally speaking, members of the hound group are also friendly, gregarious, affectionate, and loyal companions.

OPPOSITE: As well as making a lovable family pet, the Beagle is naturally adept at picking up scents.

The Irish Wolfhound is the tallest of the galloping hound breeds.

AFGHAN HOUND

As its name suggests, this sighthound hails from the mountains and plains of Afghanistan. One of the most glamorous breeds of dogs, with a regal air about it, the Afghan is in fact a powerful hunter.

The Afghan is large and dignified, but with the impression of power and speed. The head is held proudly. The skull should be long but not too narrow. The nose should be black, although liver is permissible in dogs with lighter-colored coats. Dark eyes are preferred. The ears should be carried close to the head and are covered with long, silky fur. The well-muscled, moderate-length body, with deep chest, is offset by long, strongly-boned legs, and a long tail with a ring at the tip. The coat is long and fine. Both fore and hind feet should be covered with long fur. All colors are acceptable. Intelligent and with a distinct oriental expression, these dogs appear reserved and

aloof. However, they are quite capable of playing the fool if the mood takes them. Afghans are also affectionate toward their owners, although they are one of the more demanding breeds to keep. The high-stepping gait and long, flowing coat are characteristics of this breed.

Size *Height:* dog 27–29in (68.5–74cm); bitch 25–27in (63.5–68.5cm). *Weight:* dog 60lb (27kg); bitch 50lb (23kg).

The elegant and powerful Afghan requires a good deal of exercise.

BASENJI

The Basenji has its origins in what is now the Democratic Republic of Congo, although dogs similar in appearance to this breed are found throughout central Africa and were even depicted as palace dogs at the time of the Egyptian pharaohs.

A fine-boned and lightly-built animal, the Basenji always looks poised, aristocratic, and alert. The well-chiseled, wrinkled head narrows towards the point of the nose, which should be black. The dark, almond-shaped eyes have a fixed, somewhat inscrutable expression. Ears are small, pointed, and pricked. The neck is well-arched, long, and strong. The body is short and deep, with a level back. The tail curls tightly over the back and lies to one side of the thigh in a single or a double curl.

The coat is short, smooth, and fine. Colors range from black-and-white, red-and-white, tan-and-

white, or black. There should be white present on the feet, chest, and tail tip. White legs, blaze and collar are optional.

Renowned for its cleanliness and lack of odor, the Basenji is an ideal pet. Intelligent and curious, this dog can become very bonded to its family. Basenjis do not bark, but instead make an unusual yodeling sound when they want to express themselves.

Size *Height:* dog 17in (43cm); bitch 16in (41cm).
Weight: dog 24lb (11kg); bitch 21lb (9.5kg).

The Basenji has been known to wash itself like a cat, so fastidious is it about its appearance.

BASSET HOUND

The ancestor of the Basset Hound was believed to have been bred by French monks in the Middle Ages for hunting. A close relative of the French Bassets, the breed was nevertheless developed separately in Britain by crossings with Bloodhounds. The breed was introduced to shows in Britain in 1875.

A heavily-built, slow-moving, and sometimes ponderous dog with a somewhat comical, worried expression. The long, broad head is heavily domed and bears

The Basset Hound may look mournful but is a happy and contented family dog.

long, pendulous ears. There is loose skin around the head and muzzle. The nose should be black, although it can be brown or liver in lighter-colored dogs. The eyes are brown or hazel; the red coloration of the lower lids should be visible. The low-slung body is long and with a broad, deep chest, and arched loins. Short, heavy legs end in massive feet. When moving, the long and tapering tail is held well up and slightly curving.

The coat is short and smooth, without being too fine. Usually black, white, and tan; any recognized hound color is acceptable.

This is a dog that loves to paddle through wet fields sniffing for prey – being tenacious and full of endurance – but is equally at home idling its time away by the fireside with its family.

Size *Height:* dog 12–15in (30–38cm); bitch 11–14in (28–36cm). *Weight:* dog 55–75lb (25–34kg). bitch; 45–65lb (20–29kg).

BEAGLE

The smallest of the pack hounds, the Beagle is an English breed used for hunting hares with followers on foot. The breed has been in existence since at least the reign of Henry VIII of England. The Beagle is deservedly popular in many countries including America, Britain, and France.

A bustling, active, and enthusiastic dog of compact build. The head is medium-broad with a slightly domed skull. The nose should preferably be black. The ears hang down to the cheeks and are thin, fairly long, and rounded. The eyes are brown or hazel with a friendly expression. The medium-length neck is carried on a short, deep-chested body. The

The Beagle's smooth shorthaired coat is smart and easy to maintain.

strongly-boned, muscular legs end in round feet. The tail is moderately long and carried high.

The coat is dense, short, and waterproof. Any recognized hound color is acceptable apart from liver.

Ever ready for action, the Beagle is equally happy hunting in a pack or simply being the pampered family pet. Bold, lively, and affectionate, this dog is also blessed with stamina and intelligence. The short coat is quick to wash and dry, after even the muddiest of romps. Once free of the leash, a Beagle may take off after a scent trail, seemingly deaf to its owner's calls.

Size *Height:* dog 13–16in (33–34cm); bitch 13–16in (33–34cm). *Weight:* dog 22–25lb (10–11kg). bitch; 20–23lb (9–10kg).

"You think dogs will not be in heaven? I tell you, they will be there long before any of us."
Robert Louis Stevenson (1850–1894)

BLOODHOUND

The origins of the Bloodhound can be traced back to Belgium, where legend has it that the breed was used for hunting in the Ardennes region as long ago as the 7th century. The Bloodhound was introduced to England by William the Conqueror in 1066. The name 'bloodhound' has been incorrectly attributed to the dog's legendary ability to follow a blood trail. In fact, the name is used to mean 'bloodstock' – and is a reference to aristocratic breeding.

A huge hound with great presence. The long, narrow head has characteristic hanging folds of pendulous skin, giving a somewhat lugubrious expression to the face. Eyes are brown or hazel. The long ears fall in graceful folds and feel soft to the touch. A long, throaty neck is carried on a short, deep-chested body. Long, muscular legs contribute to the dog's imposing size. The long, thick tail is carried high when on the move.

The coat is smooth, short, and waterproof. Colors are black-and tan; liver (red)-and-tan; and solid red. Small areas of white are allowed on the tail tip, chest, and feet.

Known throughout the world for its remarkable ability to follow scents and trails, the Bloodhound is a robust, powerful animal with a deep, gruff bark. Being so big, Bloodhounds can be willful unless handled correctly.

Size *Height.* dog 26in (66cm); bitch 24in (61cm). *Weight:* dog 110lb (50kg); bitch 100lb (45kg).

In films and stories, the Bloodhound is always depicted as a kind of sleuth or detective, which is due to its ability to follow a trail.

BORZOI

An ancient Russian breed, packs of Borzoi were once kept by almost all Russian noblemen. The largest Borzoi were used, in pairs, for bringing down wolves – as their original name 'Russian Wolfhound' suggests. The first Borzois seen in England were presented to Queen Alexandra by the Russian tsar.

A graceful, aristocratic dog whose body suggests great power and speed. The long, lean head has a slightly domed skull. The jaws are long and powerful and the nose is large and black. Eyes are dark, with an intelligent expression. The ears are small and pointed. The neck is slightly arched and muscular. A Borzoi's body should be comparatively short and rising to an arch at the loins, and with a deep chest. The long, narrow

The Borzoi, though the personification of elegance, is not the ideal pet for everyone.

legs are strong and muscular. The long tail is well-feathered.

The coat is silky, flat, curly, or wavy; much longer on the body and with feathering on legs, chest, hindquarters, and tail. Any color is acceptable.

Rather aloof and self-possessed, this is not by any means a typical pet dog. Some examples may be rather temperamental, and ownership should be considered carefully. The Borzoi expresses its affection for its owners but is distrustful of strangers. For such a large animal, the Borzoi does not have a huge appetite.

Size *Height:* dog 29in (74cm); bitch 27in (68.5cm). *Weight:* dog 75–105lb (34–48kg); bitch 60–90lb (27–41kg).

There was an old man of Ancona,
Who found a small dog with no owner,
Which he took up and down all the streets of the town,
That anxious old man of Ancona.
Edward Lear (1812–1888)

CIRNECO DELL'ETNA

Also known as the Sicilian Greyhound, the Cirneco dell'Etna is a small hound-type breed originating in the Italian island of Sicily. The breed is known for its endurance when used for hunting over the harsh terrain on Mount Etna. This ancient breed has had little interference and and therefore has changed little over the centuries. Today, the breed is known for its robustness and the fact that it is free from inherited disease.

The Cirneco dell'Etna is a medium-sized dog which is not only elegant and slender but also strong and hardy.

The coat is short and sleek and comes in shades of tan or chestnut. A white collar is acceptable.

Historically used for hunting rabbits, the Cirneco dell'Etna can go for hours without food and water. It is the smallest of the Mediterranean hunting hounds, the others being the Pharaoh and the Ibizan hounds. Today, it is generally kept as a pet due to its friendly nature and its low-maintenance coat. Being naturally active, however, it does require plenty of regular exercise.

Size *Height:* dog 18–20in (46–51cm); bitch 17–20in (43–51cm).
Weight: dog 22–26lb (10–12kg); bitch 18–22lb (8–10kg).

COONHOUND

In the 17th century, British colonists imported Bloodhounds into the state of Virginia in America to be used as guards for the settlements. During the second half of the 18th century, with the aid of progeny from these early Bloodhounds, dogs were bred with the intention of hunting opossums and raccoons – especially at night. These dogs were given the name of Coonhounds. Of the various Coonhounds that have been developed, the most important one is the black-and-tan variety.

A large, powerful, and alert dog with obvious Bloodhound ancestry. The head has a long, moderately-broad skull and a long, broad muzzle. The eyes are dark brown or hazel. The ears are long, pendulous, and folded. The fairly long neck is carried on a medium-length body with a deep chest. Long, well-boned legs terminate in short, powerful feet. The tail is long and held up when on the move.

The coat is short and dense. Color varies depending on the type.

Keen and ready for action, this is a dog that has been bred to withstand the cold of winter as well as the heat of summer. Coonhounds are friendly by nature but can be aggressive when required.

Size *Height:* dog 25in (63.5cm); bitch 24in (61cm). *Weight:* dog 90lb (41kg); bitch 80lb (36kg).

"Histories are more full of examples of the fidelity of dogs than of friends."

Alexander Pope (1688–1744)

The Coonhound is a large, robust dog with Bloodhound ancestry.

DACHSHUND

The word Dachshund means 'badger dog' and describes the purpose for which these tough little dogs were originally bred in their native Germany. Their short legs and powerful jaws are ideal adaptations for entering setts and taking on their quarry underground. In fact, only the larger varieties were used for hunting badgers; the smaller ones hunted stoats and weasels.

A long and low dog with a muscular body. The long, lean head has a narrow skull and a long, fine muzzle. The eyes are medium-sized, almond-shaped and colored dark reddish-brown to brown-black. The ears are broad and well-rounded and hang flat. The neck is rather long and muscular. A long body, with a deep chest and level back, must be held sufficiently clear of the ground to allow free movement. Legs are short and strong. The tail is long.

There are three distinctive coat types; *Smoothhaired:* Short, glossy, and dense. *Longhaired:* Soft and straight or slightly waved; abundant feathering on underside and behind legs. *Wirehaired:* Whole body, except for the chin, ears, jaws, and eyebrows are covered with short, straight, harsh hair. All colors are permissible.

Intelligent and lively, Dachshunds need firm training to curb disobedience. Despite their small size, they make admirable watchdogs and are fearless in the protection of their family and friends, to whom they are very loyal.

Size *Weight:* large varieties 26lb (12kg); small varieties 10lb (4.5kg).

Because they are so near to the ground, care should be taken not to step on the little Dachshund.

GREYHOUND

Many experts believe that the Greyhound has its origins in the Middle East, in that images of dogs resembling Greyhounds have been found on the walls of Ancient Egyptian tombs dating back to 4000BC. The racing Greyhound is slightly smaller than the show dog. Racing Greyhounds have been measured at speeds of over 45mph (72kph), making them one of the fastest of all animals.

A strongly-built, muscular, and symmetrical animal. The head is long with a broad skull and a long, strong muzzle. The dark eyes bear an intelligent expression. The ears are small and rose-shaped. The neck is long and muscular. A deep and capacious chest allows for plenty of heart room. The back is long with powerful muscles, and there are slightly arched loins. Long, strongly-boned legs terminate in long feet. The tail is long.

The fine coat lies close to the body. Colors may be black, white, red, fawn, brindle or fallow, or any combination of these colors with white.

Greyhounds possess remarkable endurance and stamina and, of course, a turn of speed second to none in the canine world, which is facilitated by the animal's long-reaching movement over the ground. Greyhounds are quiet, calm, and affectionate dogs – although with a natural desire to chase other, smaller animals. Nevertheless, they make good companions and pets.

Size *Height:* dog 28–30in (71–76cm); bitch 27–28in (68.5–71cm). *Weight:* dog 65–70lb (29–32kg); bitch 60–65lb (27–29kg).

A Greyhound's racing days can be short-lived, but with correct handling, they make excellent pets once retired.

IBIZAN HOUND

In the tomb of the Pharaoh Hemako was found a carved dish bearing an image of an Ibizan Hound. The dish was made in the 1st Dynasty, between 3100 and 2700BC, thus indicating that the history of this breed can be traced back at least to the time of the Ancient Egyptians. The breed takes its name from the Balearic island of Ibiza, and was probably taken there by Phoenician traders. It has been known on the island, and on nearby Formentera, for 5,000 years at least.

A finely-built dog with upright ears. The head has a long, narrow skull, and muzzle. The nose is flesh-colored. Eyes are amber and fairly small. The ears are large and pricked. A long, lean neck is carried on a body with a long, flat ribcage, and arched loins. The legs are long and strong and terminate in hare feet. The tail is long and thin.

The coat may be smooth or rough but always dense and hard; it is longer under the tail. The color can be white, 'lion' color; or any combination of these colors.

A renowned jumper, this breed needs plenty of room to exercise. Sometimes aloof with strangers, the Ibizan Hound is nevertheless devoted to its owner. It is also intelligent, cheerful and non-aggressive.

Size *Height:* 22–29in (56–74cm). *Weight:* dog 49lb (22kg); bitch 42lb (19kg).

IRISH WOLFHOUND

Perhaps no other dog evokes such looks of admiration as the Irish Wolfhound. This magnificent breed was known to the Ancient Romans, and it was held in great esteem from the 12th to the 16th centuries in Ireland, where it was used to hunt wolf, bear, stag, and elk. When the last wolf was wiped out in Ireland, the Irish Wolfhound almost became extinct as well. In the mid-19th century, however, the breed was revived using the few remaining specimens.

Of commanding size, and appearance, coupled with muscular

strength. The head is long, and the skull not too broad. The muzzle is long and moderately pointed. The nose is black. The eyes are dark. The small rose ears have a fine, velvety texture. The neck is long and muscular. A long body with a very deep chest and arched loins is carried on long, well-boned legs. The tail is long and slightly curved.

The coat is rough, hard and shaggy; long and wiry over the eyes and under the jaw. Colors are black, gray, red, brindle, fawn, wheaten, steel-gray, or pure white.

The breed's comparative rarity and huge size, together with its air of dignity, set it apart from others.

Size *Height:* dog 31in (79cm); bitch 28in (71cm). *Weight:* dog 120lb (54kg); bitch 90lb (41kg).

The Irish Wolfhound is an ancient breed, known for its huge size and dignified appearance.

PHARAOH HOUND

The paintings on pottery and other artifacts found in the tombs of the Ancient Egyptians clearly depict dogs almost identical to the Pharaoh Hound known today. It is thought that the breed then came to Malta from Africa with Phoenician traders. It was from this island that the breed was introduced elsewhere, and it arrived in Britain, for example, in the 1970s.

A graceful-looking dog with a noble bearing. The head has a long skull and a long muzzle with a slight stop. The small, amber-colored eyes are oval and have an intelligent expression. The ears are pricked. A long, lean, and strong neck is carried on a long body with a deep

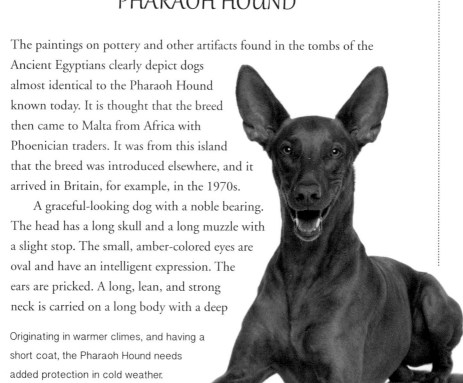

Originating in warmer climes, and having a short coat, the Pharaoh Hound needs added protection in cold weather.

chest. The legs are also long and well-boned. The long tail is held high and curved on the move.

The coat is fine or slightly harsh; short and glossy. The color is basically rich tan but with a white tail tip, white mark on the chest and white toes. A slim white blaze on the center of the face is also acceptable.

An alert hunter that tracks its prey by both scent and sight, this is a true working hound. However, the Pharaoh Hound is also friendly and affectionate, and willing to play.

Size *Height:* dog 22–25in (56–63.5cm); bitch 21–24in (53–61cm).
Weight: dog 44–45lb (20kg).

"A dog reflects the family life. Whoever saw a frisky dog in a gloomy family, or a sad dog in a happy one? Snarling people have snarling dogs, dangerous people have dangerous ones."

Sir Arthur Conan Doyle (1859–1930)

RHODESIAN RIDGEBACK

The Rhodesian Ridgeback was developed by crossing dogs brought to Southern Africa by European farmers with native hunting dogs. This produced a large breed of dog that was ideal for hunting game and also for guarding. The original native dogs had a ridge on their back, and this feature is a characteristic of the Rhodesian Ridgeback. The dog was introduced to Rhodesia (now Zimbabwe) in the 1870s and was given the name of that country, having been bred there in large numbers.

The head has a broad skull with a long, deep muzzle. The nose is black or brown. The eyes are round and bright and should tone with the coat color. The medium-sized ears are pendulous. The muscular body is fairly long and supports a long, strong neck. The legs are strong and muscular. The tail is carried with a slight upward curve but never curled.

The coat is short and dense, with a glossy, sleek appearance; the ridge of hair on the back should be clearly defined, tapering and symmetrical. Color is light wheaten to red wheaten, with only small amounts of white on the chest and toes.

Powerful and agile, the Rhodesian Ridgeback is a loyal and protective dog towards its family, although it is not necessarily an ideal choice for the inexperienced dog owner.

Size *Height:* dog 25–27in (63.5–68.5cm); bitch 24–26in (61–66cm). *Weight:* dog 80lb (36kg); bitch 70lb (32kg).

The Rhodesian Ridgeback is loyal and protective, but requires proper training and correct handling.

SALUKI

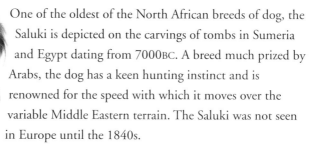

One of the oldest of the North African breeds of dog, the Saluki is depicted on the carvings of tombs in Sumeria and Egypt dating from 7000BC. A breed much prized by Arabs, the dog has a keen hunting instinct and is renowned for the speed with which it moves over the variable Middle Eastern terrain. The Saluki was not seen in Europe until the 1840s.

The overall impression is of grace and speed. The long, narrow head tapers towards the nose, which is black or liver. The muzzle is long and strong. The large eyes are dark to light-brown in color, with an intelligent, interested expression. The long, mobile ears are covered with long, silky fur. The body, like the neck, is long. The chest is deep with slightly arched ribs. Long, powerful legs and feet and a long, well-feathered tail complement the other features.

The coat is soft and silky, longer on the ears, with feathering on legs, backs of thighs, and tail. Colors are white, cream, fawn, red, grizzle, silver grizzle, tricolor (black, white and tan), black-and-tan, and permutations of these colors.

A speedy and active hunter with a far-seeing gaze. Although somewhat reserved with strangers, and even highly-strung, the dog is very affectionate towards its owner.

Size *Height:* dog 23–28in (58.5–71cm); bitch proportionately smaller. *Weight:* 40–60lb (18–27kg).

THE YELPERS

Johann Wolfgang von Goethe (1749–1832)

Our rides in all directions bend,

For business or for pleasure,
Yet yelpings on our steps attend,

And barkings without measure.
The dog that in our stable dwells,

After our heels is striding,
And all the while his noisy yells
But show that we are riding.

The Saluki is the oldest of the African breeds and has been depicted on ancient artifacts.

WHIPPET

Despite appearances, the Whippet is not a small Greyhound. It came about in the 19th century when it was made legal in Britain for working people to hunt small game and vermin. Originally called a 'snap-dog,' the term may have been coined either because of the animal's ability to snap up small game such as rabbits, or because of the English word 'snap', meaning food – a reference to the dog's ability to provide food for its owner.

Muscular and powerful, but at the same time graceful and elegant. The head is long and lean with a

48

tapering muzzle. The nose should be black or of a color toning with the body color. The oval eyes are bright and lively. The ears are fine and rose-shaped. A long, well-muscled neck is supported by a fairly long body with a deep chest and arched loins; the loins should give an impression of power and muscularity. The legs are long and strong. The tail is long and tapering.

The coat is fine, dense, and short. Any color or mixture of colors is permissable.

A highly adaptable sporting dog that is happy out in the field, at home with the family, or trotting at heel to the shops. A deservedly popular animal, it is both gentle and affectionate.

Size *Height:* dog 18.5–20in (47–51cm); bitch 17–18.5in (43–47cm). *Weight:* 27.5–30lb (12.5–13.5kg).

A highly valued sporting dog, the Whippet has a wonderful disposition, and makes an excellent pet.

THE SPORTING GROUP

Dogs in this group were all bred to assist in the hunting and retrieving of game. As early as the 6th century BC, there were records of certain types of dog which, instead of pursuing game, sniffed the scent with raised head and then stood completely still. Although originally considered a rather unsatisfactory characteristic in a hunting dog, it was later realized that the behavior could, in fact, be very useful in the right circumstances. This was particularly the case when hunters wanted to net partridge or quail, for example. Then, the dogs were trained to crouch, sit or lie down when they had spotted game so that the hunters could draw a net over the birds before they were able to fly away.

A Springer Spaniel.

OPPOSITE: A German Pointer.

Among the features exhibited by many gundogs are weatherproof coats that enable them to work in often cold, wet conditions, including freezing water. In order to respond consistently and obediently to commands, gundogs must usually be loyal, willing to please, and friendly by nature – features that makes this group the most popular of all in terms of human companions and family pets. The stealthy nature of their work also means that they are less given to vocalization than hounds; again, a considerable attribute in a housedog.

Among the gundogs, different breeds are used for the various tasks in the field. The gundogs that exemplify pointing behavior include the various breeds of pointer (such as the Pointer and the English Setter). Dogs such as the Springer Spaniel are prized for their ability to flush game from cover; some will also

A Golden Retriever.

OPPOSITE: A Weimaraner.

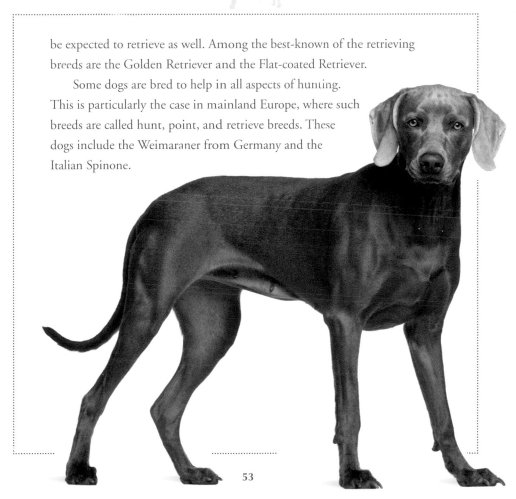

be expected to retrieve as well. Among the best-known of the retrieving breeds are the Golden Retriever and the Flat-coated Retriever.

Some dogs are bred to help in all aspects of hunting. This is particularly the case in mainland Europe, where such breeds are called hunt, point, and retrieve breeds. These dogs include the Weimaraner from Germany and the Italian Spinone.

BRITTANY

Originally French, the Brittany is another hunt, point, and retrieve breed. The dog was once known as the Brittany Spaniel, and although this is a true French spaniel, it is really more like a small setter. These good-natured and friendly dogs have gained popularity in America and will likely increase their fan club in Britain, too.

Compact and square-looking with a medium-length skull and well-defined stop. The muzzle is tapered. The expressive eyes are brown, harmonizing with the coat color. The drop ears are set high and are rather short. The medium-length neck is carried on a deep-chested body with a short, slightly sloping back. The legs are fairly well-boned, long,

The Brittany is famous as much for its abilities in the field as it is for its charm.

and muscular, and the feet are small. These dogs are often born tailless, but when tails are present they are kept short or docked.

The coat is flat and dense; fine, and wavy. Colors are orange-and-white, liver-and-white, black-and-white, tricolor, or a roan of any of these colors.

This active and energetic dog is keen to please and therefore easy to train. A good worker in the field, being able to hunt, point, and retrieve, the Brittany is both intelligent and affectionate.

Size *Height:* dog 19–20in (48–51cm); bitch 18–19in (46–48cm). *Weight:* 30–40lb (13.5–18kg).

"If a dog will not come to you after having looked you in the face, you should go home and examine your conscience."

Woodrow Wilson (1856–1924)

CHESAPEAKE BAY RETRIEVER

During the early part of the 19th century, two puppies, reported as Newfoundland in type, were rescued from a shipwreck off the coast of Maryland, USA. These dogs were mated with local retrievers and the crossings were the start of the breed known as the Chesapeake Bay Retriever. The dog was used to retrieve ducks in the cold waters of Chesapeake Bay, being suitably adapted for this purpose by virtue of its thick, oily, waterproof coat.

A strong, muscular dog with a distinctive coat. The skull is broad with a shortish, relatively broad muzzle. The nose color should harmonize with the coat. The eyes should be yellow or amber. The small ears hang loosely at the sides of the head, the muscular neck tapering from the head to the shoulders. The body is of medium length with a deep chest. The strong, medium-length legs terminate in webbed hare-feet. The tail is heavy and strong and should be straight or slightly curved.

The coat is short and thick with a dense, woolly undercoat. It should be oily and able to resist water. Colors can range from dark brown to faded tan or the color of dead grass.

Essentially a duck dog, and in its element when in the water, this is a willing, courageous and independent dog.

Size *Height:* dog 23–26in (58.5–66cm); bitch 21–24in (53–61cm). *Weight:* dog 65–80lb (29–36kg); bitch 55–70lb (25–32kg).

The Chesapeake Bay is a hardy outdoor type and probably the most talented of the duck dogs.

AMERICAN COCKER SPANIEL

This attractive-looking dog was bred in America in the 19th century from Cocker Spaniels imported from Britain, its main job being to retrieve gamebirds such as quail. The smallest of the sporting group, the American Cocker Spaniel is a sound and willing worker.

A distinctive, smallish, neat dog with a full coat on the legs and abdomen. The head is shortish and refined, with a rounded skull and a deep, broad muzzle. The nose should be black in black-and-tans and brown or black in dogs of other colors. The eyes are full and round, with a forward-looking gaze; the expression should be alert and appealing. The ears are long and lobe-shaped and should be covered with long fur. The neck is long and muscular. The body is short and compact with a deep chest; the back slopes slightly from withers to tail. The legs are strong and muscular. The tail is usually docked by three-fifths of its length.

The medium-length coat is silky and flat or slightly wavy; shorter on the head. The dog comes in various colors, including solid black and black-and-tan.

A keen and happy dog with a friendly and confident manner, the breed makes an excellent family pet.

Size *Height:* dog 14.5–15.5in (37–39.5cm);
bitch 13.5–14.5in (34–37cm).
Weight: 24–28.5lb (11–13kg).

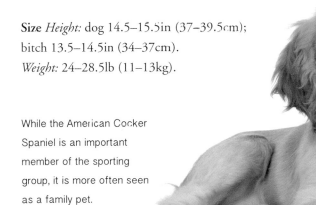

While the American Cocker Spaniel is an important member of the sporting group, it is more often seen as a family pet.

CURLY-COATED RETRIEVER

This breed arose as the result of crossings between water spaniels, various sorts of retrievers and, possibly, poodles. The tight, curly coat was probably enhanced by adding poodle stock to the breeding program. The unique coat is well-adapted for work in water and is quick-drying.

A strong, elegant-looking dog with a dark, curly coat, the head is long and wedge-shaped with a fairly broad skull and longish

The Curly-coated Retriever is the result of crossing water spaniels, retrievers, and possibly, poodles.

muzzle. The nose is black in dogs with black fur and brown in brown-coated dogs. The eyes are large and, again, should harmonize with the coat color. The pendulous ears are rather small and lie close to the head. The strong neck is carried on a broad body with a deep chest. The legs are strong and muscular and terminate in round feet. The tail is long.

The coat is a mass of small, tight curls extending over most of the body apart from the face and skull. Colors are black or liver.

In the field, the Curly-coated Retriever is adept at marking where fallen game is lying and retrieving it. An intelligent dog, with great stamina and confidence, the breed is happiest when leading an active life.

Size *Height:* dog 27in (68.5cm); bitch 25in (63.5cm). *Weight:* 70–80lb (32–36kg).

ENGLISH COCKER SPANIEL

One of the oldest spaniel breeds, the dog's original name of Cocking Spaniel derived from it being used to flush woodcocks from cover in woods and marshes. Soon after the Kennel Club formed in 1873, Cocker Spaniels were recognized as a separate breed from Springer Spaniels and Field Spaniels.

The overall impression is of a merry, compact, well-balanced sporting dog. The skull should not be too broad or long, and the muzzle should be square with a distinct stop. The eyes are dark-brown or lighter brown or hazel, toning with the coat; the expression is intelligent, alert, and gentle. The ears are lobe-shaped, thin, and pendulous. A muscular, moderate-length neck is carried on a strong, compact body with a well-developed chest. The dog has short, strongly-boned legs, and cat-feet.

The tail is usually docked, but never so short that it impedes its non-stop action when on the move.

The coat is flat and silky; well-feathered fore legs, hind legs (above hocks), and body. Various colors are available; self-colors should only have white on the chest.

Willing and happy, the Cocker Spaniel is quick to adapt to its surroundings and is equally at home sniffing around in the countryside as it is playing indoors with its family.

Size *Height:* dog 15.5–16in (39.5–41cm); bitch 15–15.5in (38–39.5cm). *Weight:* 28–32lb (13–14.5kg).

The English Cocker is full of charm matched with good looks and a lively personality.

ENGLISH SETTER

One of the oldest sporting breeds, and also one of the most stylish and admired, the English Setter shows evidence of a mixed ancestry involving pointers and spaniels.

A dog with clean, elegant lines, and a smooth movement. The head is long with a moderately broad skull and a moderately deep and square muzzle. The nose should be black or liver, depending on the coat color. The bright, expressive eyes can be hazel to dark brown. The ears are moderately long and hang in folds. A rather long, muscular neck is carried on a body of moderate length with well-rounded ribs. The legs are strong, muscular, and well-boned. The tail is medium-length and carried with a lively movement.

The coat is wavy, long, and silky; shorter on the head, and with a well-feathered tail, breeches, and fore

The elegant English Setter requires a good deal of exercise.

legs. Colors are black-and-white (known as blue belton), orange-and-white (known as orange belton), lemon-and-white (known as lemon belton), liver-and-white (known as liver belton), or tricolor (known as blue belton-and-tan, or liver belton-and-tan).

A dog that excels at its task in the field, quartering the ground at speed and then setting rapidly when the quarry is located. This breed also makes a first-rate companion and pet.

Size *Height:* dog 25.5–27in (65–68.5cm); bitch 24–25.5in (61–65cm). *Weight:* dog 60–66lb (27–30kg); bitch 56–62lb (25–28kg).

"A bone to the dog is not charity. Charity is the bone shared with the dog, when you are just as hungry as the dog."

Jack London (1876–1916)

ENGLISH SPRINGER SPANIEL

Formerly known as the Norfolk Spaniel, this pure and ancient breed was awarded official status in 1902. The breed gets the name 'springer' from the fact that the type was used to flush birds into the air from cover so that they would spring upwards and thus be bagged by the shooters.

A compact, racy dog of symmetrical build that stands high on the leg. The medium-length skull is fairly broad, and the muzzle is rather broad and deep. The almond-shaped eyes, of hazel coloration, have a kind and alert expression. The ears are lobe-shaped, fairly long, and hang flat. The neck is rather long, strong, and muscular. The body is strong with a deep chest and is carried on well-developed legs. The tail, customarily docked, is well-feathered and has a lively action.

The coat is long, dense, and soft but also tough and weather-resistant; feathering on ears, fore legs, belly, and hindquarters. Colors are black-and-white, liver-and-white, or these colors with tan markings.

A friendly and extrovert gundog, willing to search for, flush, and retrieve game – even in icy water. An affectionate family dog, too, but one that likes plenty of exercise.

Size *Height:* dog 18–20in (46–51cm); bitch 17–19in (43–48cm). *Weight:* dog 50–55lb (23–25kg); bitch 35–45lb (18–18kg).

Ideally, the English Springer needs plenty of space to run and somewhere safe to swim.

FLAT-COATED RETRIEVER

A blend of the St John's Newfoundland (a smaller version of the Newfoundland) and spaniels, setters and sheepdogs, the breed was first shown in Britain in 1859. Less popular than other types of gundog for some years, there is now growing interest in the Flat-coated Retriever, which has the lightest build of all the retrievers.

The Flat-coated Retriever is naturally playful and also a keen swimmer.

A medium-sized dog with an intelligent expression and an active nature. The head is long, with a medium-broad skull, and a longish muzzle. The eyes are dark-brown to hazel. The ears are small and close-fitting to the sides of the head. The body has a rather broad, deep chest. Moderately-long, strongly-boned legs terminate in rounded feet with thick pads. The tail is fairly short and carried jauntily, though seldom above the level of the back.

The coat is dense, of fine to medium texture, and should be as flat as possible. Colors are black or liver.

The Flat-coated Retriever matures slowly, retaining its puppy-like nature for years. This is a cheerful and playful extrovert that enjoys the companionship of humans, yet makes a good guard dog when needed.

Size *Height:* dog 23–24in (58.5–61cm); bitch 22–23in (56–58.5cm). *Weight:* dog 60–80lb (27–36kg); bitch 55–70lb (25–32kg).

GERMAN SHORTHAIRED POINTER

The origins of this breed probably stem from the stock owned by Prince Albert zu Somsbrauenfels – which were worthy but rather slow German gundogs. These were crossed with English Pointer stock, with the result that the excellent scenting ability of the German dogs was now combined with more spirited English qualities to produce a highly versatile hunt, point, and retrieve gundog.

A well-balanced animal displaying power, endurance, and symmetry. The head is lean and clean-cut with a broad skull and a long, strong muzzle. Depending on the coat color, the nose should be solid brown or black. The brown eyes are medium-sized, with a soft and intelligent expression. The moderately long ears hang down flat. A fairly long neck is carried on a deep-chested body with a firm, short back, and slightly arched loins. The legs are strong and well-boned. The tail is usually docked to medium length.

The coat is short, dense, and flat. Colors are solid black or solid liver, or both coat colors may be spotted or ticked with white.

An aristocratic-looking dog conveying the impression of alertness and energy. These are dual-purpose pointer/retrievers with keen noses and great perseverance in the field.

Size *Height:* dog 23–25in (58.5–63.5cm); bitch 21–23in (53–58.5cm). *Weight:* dog 55–70lb (25–32kg); bitch 45–60lb (20–27kg).

The German Shorthaired Pointer is a versatile all-rounder. They make good pets but need plenty of exercise.

GERMAN WIREHAIRED POINTER

Created by selectively breeding certain German gundog breeds with the German Shorthair, this attractive and hardy character is a little bigger than its shorthaired cousin. This is another hunt, point, and retrieve breed.

The head is moderately long with a broad skull. The nose is liver or black. The medium-sized oval eyes are hazel or a darker shade. The medium-sized, rounded ears hang down. A strong neck is carried on a deep-chested body with a firm back that falls slightly towards the rear. The legs are strong and muscular. The tail is customarily docked to medium length, and is held horizontally when the animal is on the move.

The outercoat is harsh and thick and weather-resistant; the undercoat is dense. Bushy eyebrows and a full beard are desirable features. Colors are liver-and-white, liver, or black-and-white.

A strong, wirehaired hunting breed equally capable of working in water as over ground. An alert, intelligent and steady dog, it is also loyal, and affectionate and good in the house. Being essentially a working breed, regular exercise is an important requirement.

Size *Height:* dog 24–26in (61–66cm); bitch 22–24in (56–61cm). *Weight:* dog 55–75lb (25–34kg); bitch 45–64lb (20–29kg).

GOLDEN RETRIEVER

The Golden Retriever is thought to have been created from first crossing a yellow wavy-coated retriever with a spaniel, and then mating it on with setters and other retrievers. These dogs were first known as Retrievers (Golden or Yellow), but in 1920 took their present name of Golden Retriever.

The head has a broad skull with a powerful, wide, deep muzzle. The nose should be black. The eyes are dark-brown and have a kindly expression. The ears are moderately large and hang flat. A clean, muscular neck is carried on a shortish body with deep ribs. The legs are moderately long and

Its even temperament makes the Golden Retriever one of the most versatile of dogs and a favorite family pet.

74

well-boned, and the feet are round and cat-like. The muscular tail is carried level with the back; it is used for steering when swimming.

The coat should be flat or wavy and well-feathered; the undercoat is dense and water-resistant. The color may be any shade of cream or gold.

An intelligent dog with natural ability, the Golden Retriever is easy to train.

Size *Height:* dog 22–24in (56–61cm); bitch 20–22in (51–56cm). *Weight:* dog 70–80lb (32–36kg); bitch 60–70lb (27–32kg).

"Does not the gratitude of the dog put to shame any man who is ungrateful to his benefactors?"

St Basil

GORDON SETTER

As its name implies, the Gordon Setter is of Scottish origin and was bred to perfection by the Duke of Gordon in the late 18th century. Because the breed is somewhat less fashionable than the Irish or English Setters, the Gordon Setter has remained a no-nonsense, steady, working gundog.

A well-built, stylish-looking dog with a glossy coat. The head is more deep than broad, with a moderately broad skull and a long, almost square-ended muzzle. The nose is black. The eyes are dark-brown and intelligent-looking. The ears are medium-length and pendulous. The neck is long, and carried on a short, deep body with slightly arched loins. Strong, moderately-long, well-boned legs terminate in oval feet. The tail is long and tapers to the tip.

The coat should be soft and glossy, straight, or slightly wavy. The hair on the ears, under the stomach and chest, back of legs and under the tail is long. The color is coal-black with rich reddish-tan markings.

The Gordon Setter is heavier, and less swift, than the English or Irish Setters. A bold and outgoing dog, the Gordon Setter is capable, trustworthy and intelligent, with an even disposition.

Size *Height:* dog 26in (66cm); bitch 24.5in (62cm). *Weight:* dog 65lb (29kg); bitch 56lb (25kg).

A natural pointer and retriever, the Gordon Setter also makes a delightful pet.

IRISH SETTER

This is one of the most glamorous of dog breeds, with its striking chestnut coat. The dashing Irish Setter, often called the Red Setter, increased in popularity from the late 1800s on, although little is known concerning the true origins of the breed.

A sleek and handsome dog with a racy appearance. The head is long and lean, with a fairly narrow, oval skull, and a long, almost square muzzle. The nose is dark-brown to black. The kindly-looking eyes are dark-brown. The ears are of medium

The Irish Setter is an active and spirited breed, so requires plenty of space to run free.

length and hang in a neat fold close to the head. The muscular neck is carried on a deep-chested, rather narrow body. The legs are fairly long and strongly boned. The tail should be fairly long and in proportion with the body size; it is carried level with the back, or just below, when on the move.

The coat is of moderate length, flat, and free from waviness or curl, if possible; short and fine on the head, front of legs and ear-tips; feathering on upper parts of ears, backs of legs; longer hair on belly and tail. Color is a rich chestnut red with no traces of black.

Despite the Irish Setter's refined appearance, this is an active, willing, and able sporting dog, with a carefree nature. The breed is hugely popular as a pet, thanks to its affectionate and playful nature.

Size *Height:* dog 27in (68.5cm); bitch 23in (58.5cm).
Weight: dog 70lb (32kg); bitch 60lb (27kg).

ITALIAN SPINONE

One of the many Continental hunt, point, and retrieve breeds, the Italian Spinone has a very old ancestry made up of native Italian hounds crossed with French Griffons among others. The Spinone is used especially for hunting in woodland and marshy country.

A solid-looking dog with a benign expression. The head is long with a flattish skull and a squarish muzzle. The large eyes are yellow, orange, or ochre, depending on the coat color. The triangular ears are pendulous and covered with short, thick hair. The neck is strong and short. The body is short and deep with a broad chest. The legs are long and well-boned. The tail is thick but usually docked to half its length.

The coat is thick and close-lying but slightly tough and wiry; pronounced eyebrows, moustache, and beard. Colors are white, or white with orange or chestnut patches or spots.

A strong, all-purpose gundog with a winning nature. Easy to train, the Italian Spinone has also proved itself to be a trustworthy and affectionate family dog.

Size *Height:* dog 23.5–27.5in (60–70cm); bitch 23–25.5in (58.5–65cm). *Weight:* dog 70–82lb (32–37kg); bitch 62–71lb (28–32kg).

LABRADOR RETRIEVER

The Labrador Retriever is believed to have its origins in Greenland, where similar dogs were once used by fishermen to retrieve fish. It was introduced into Britain in the late 1800s and made its reputation in field trials. The breed club for these dogs was started comparatively recently, in 1916, with the Yellow Labrador club being formed in 1925. Today it is one of the best-known and popular breeds in the world.

Instantly recognizable, the overall impression is of a strongly-built, active dog. The head has a broad skull with a broad, medium-length muzzle. The eyes are brown or hazel, and should express intelligence and good nature. The ears are set fairly far back on the head and hang flat. The strong neck is carried on a body with a broad, deep chest. The legs are well-developed. The tail is thick and broad and covered in short, dense fur, giving it a rounded appearance.

The distinctive coat is short and dense and feels fairly hard to the touch; the undercoat is waterproof. Colors may be solid black, yellow, or liver.

An intelligent, soft-mouthed retriever with a willingness to work and a love of water and the countryside.

Size *Height:* dog 22–22.5in (56–57cm); bitch 21.5–22in (54.5–56cm). *Weight:* dog 60–75lb (27–34kg); bitch 55–70lb (25–32kg).

The Labrador Retriever is a capable and energetic dog, eager to work and play with enthusiasm.

NOVA SCOTIA DUCK-TOLLING RETRIEVER

The Nova Scotia Duck-Tolling Retriever originated in Canada, the first examples of this breed arriving in Britain in 1988. The dog has been bred selectively to enhance the trait of intelligence. In the field, the dog waves its profuse, white-tipped tail to attract ducks and other waterfowl within range of the hunters' guns and then retrieves the kills.

A richly-colored dog of compact and powerful appearance. The skull is wedge-shaped, broad and slightly rounded, and the muzzle tapers from stop to nose, which may be black or flesh-colored. The medium-sized eyes are brown or amber. The triangular-shaped ears are held slightly erect at their base. The neck is of moderate length and well-muscled. The deep-chested body has a short back and strong, muscular loins. The legs are strong and muscular and terminate in round, strongly webbed feet – an adaptation for swimming. The tail is well-feathered and held curled over the back when alert.

A medium-length, double coat with a softer undercoat. The hair is straight and water-repellent. There is feathering on the throat, behind the ears, at the back of the thighs and on the fore legs. Color may be any shade of orange or red, with lighter tail feathering; white tips to the tail, feet and chest are permitted.

A powerful swimmer and tracker, the Nova Scotia Duck-Tolling Retriever, or Duck-Toller as it is often known, also makes a playful and friendly pet.

Size *Height:* dog 19–20in (48–51cm); bitch 18–19in (46–48cm).
Weight: 37.5–51lb (17–23kg).

The Nova Scotia Duck-Tolling Retriever has a rich, waterproof coat and powerful build.

POINTER

The Pointer is thought to have originated in Spain but was used in Britain from the mid-17th century to indicate, by pointing, where game was lying up. In the early 18th century, when guns came into more general use, the Pointer was further bred to improve its ability as a gundog. Excellent scenting powers, a speedy action over the ground, and a steadiness when pointing, are all traits desirable in the modern-day Pointer.

The breed should give the impression of compact power, agility and alertness. The head is aristocratic with a moderately-broad skull and a long muzzle with concave nose bridge. The kindly eyes are brown or hazel, according to the coat color. The ears are medium-length and hang down. The neck is long, round, and strong. The body is short and fairly broad with a deep chest carried on moderately-long, strongly-boned legs. The tail is medium-length and swings from side to side when the dog is on the move.

The coat is short, fine, and hard with a sheen. Colors are lemon-and-white, orange-and-white, liver-and-white, and black-and-white. Solid colors and tricolors are also allowed.

An enthusiastic and able worker with great powers of speed and endurance. The Pointer also fits in well with family life.

Size *Height:* dog 25–27in (63.5–68.5cm); bitch 24–26in (61–66cm). *Weight:* dog 65lb (29.5kg); bitch 57.5lb (26kg).

The Pointer is well-behaved, versatile, and athletic. It is also an excellent watchdog.

VIZSLA

A native of the plains of central Hungary, the Vizsla is also sometimes called the Hungarian Pointer. The breed suffered as a result of wars in 20th-century Europe, but it was brought back from the point of extinction to become a first-class gundog – particularly in water – and to enjoy considerable show success in Britain and America.

Medium-sized and of distinctive and powerful appearance, the head is lean and muscular and there is a moderately long skull and muzzle. The nose is brown. The slightly oval eyes should tone in color with the coat. The ears are fairly large, rounded V-shaped and pendulous. The neck is moderately long and muscular. The back is short and well-muscled, and the chest is moderately deep. The legs are fairly long and well-boned. The tail is fairly thick, and it is customarily docked to two-thirds its length.

The coat is short, smooth, dense, and glossy. The color is rusty gold.

A lively and intelligent dog with great stamina, the Hungarian Vizsla is an excellent general-purpose gundog, combining a good nose with stable pointing and reliable retrieving skills. The breed also makes a gentle, affectionate, and protective pet, adapting itself to all kinds of homes.

Size *Height:* dog 22.5–25in (57–63.5cm); bitch 21–23.5in (53–60cm). *Weight:* 48.5–66lb (22–30kg).

WEIMARANER

The Weimaraner gets its name from the German court of Weimar, where the dog was very popular. Dogs of similar appearance, albeit more houndlike, appear in paintings from the early 1600s by Van Dyck. The dog has proved effective in hunt, point, and retrieve duties. Originally, it was used to hunt boar and deer, but today usually accompanies hunters looking for smaller game. The most commonly seen version of this dog is the shorthaired variety, although there is also a longhaired form.

A tall, elegant and purposeful-looking dog with an unusual coloration. The head is fairly long and aristocratic with a long muzzle. The nose is gray. The eyes are round and vary in color from amber to blue-gray. The ears are long, taper to a point,

The Weimaraner is tall, sophisticated, confident, and assertive.

and are slightly folded. A moderately-long neck is carried on a rather long body with a deep chest, and the legs are strong and well-boned. The tail is docked.

The coat is short and sleek. In the longhaired variety, the fur is 1–2 inches (2.5–5cm) long, with feathering on the tail and back of the limbs. Color is silver-gray, mouse-gray, or roe-gray with a metallic sheen.

An able multi-role hunting dog which is fearless but friendly and obedient. The breed is increasingly finding favor as a companion.

Size *Height:* dog 24–27in (61–68.5cm); bitch 22–25in (56–63.5cm). *Weight:* dog 59.5lb (27kg); bitch 49.5lb (22.5kg).

"The greatest pleasure of a dog is that you may make a fool of yourself with him, and not only will he not scold you, but he will make a fool of himself, too."
Samuel Butler (1835–1902)

WELSH SPRINGER SPANIEL

Red-and-white spaniels closely resembling the Welsh have existed for many years. The Welsh Springer Spaniel was recognized by the Kennel Club in 1902. Slightly lighter in build than the English Springer, the Welsh was used extensively for hunting but nowadays is seen increasingly at shows.

A compact and attractively marked dog, similar to, but slightly smaller than the English Springer. The head is of moderate length, with a slightly domed skull and a medium-length muzzle. The nose is flesh-colored or darker. The eyes are hazel or dark-brown with a kindly expression. The ears are fairly small and hang flat. The neck is long and muscular. The body is not long but is strong and muscular. Medium-length, well-boned legs terminate in round, cat-like feet. The tail is usually docked and has a lively action.

The coat is straight, thick, and silky; feathering occurs on the fore legs, hind legs above the hocks, ears, and tail. Color is rich red-and-white.

A dog built to work hard and without tiring, being fast, and active. The Welsh Springer Spaniel also makes an obedient and friendly house pet.

Size *Height:* dog 19in (48cm); bitch 18in (46cm). *Weight:* 34–45lb (15–20kg).

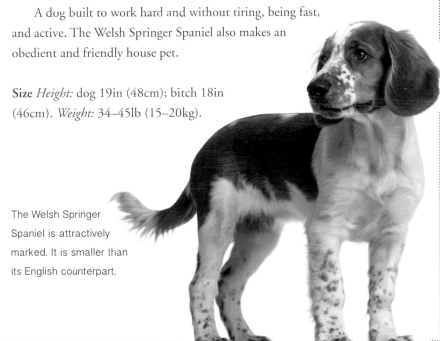

The Welsh Springer Spaniel is attractively marked. It is smaller than its English counterpart.

WIREHAIRED POINTING GRIFFON

The Wirehaired Pointing Griffon is also known as the Korthals Griffon in Germany and as the Griffon d'Arrêt à Poil Dur in France and Québec. It is bred to cover all terrains when out hunting and its superb temperament and trainability has earned it the nickname of 'supreme gundog.' The breed is sometimes taken to be Dutch in ancestry, due to the nationality of the breed founder, Eduard Karel Korthals. But it was first established in Germany and then

The Wirehaired Pointing Griffon is a friendly dog and is also very intelligent and trainable.

later in France. The breed is still relatively rare in the United States, Canada, and the United Kingdom.

The Wirehaired Pointing Griffon is a medium-sized dog with a square-shaped head and powerful limbs. Its movement is graceful, demonstrating a noble and powerful presence.

The coat is coarse, rather than soft, but has a thick undercoat of fine, soft hair. The coat is usually steel-gray with brown markings, although other colors, such as chestnut-brown, white-and-brown, roan-and-white, and orange are also acceptable.

The Wirehaired Pointing Griffon is intelligent and extremely eager to please, with the result that it responds well to kindness and is very trainable. It loves human companionship and is happiest when living alongside its owner.

Size *Height:* dog 23–24in (58–61cm); bitch 20–22in (51–56cm). *Weight:* dog 60lb (27kg); bitch 50lb (23kg).

THE TERRIER GROUP

The word 'terrier' comes from *terra*, the Latin word for earth, and aptly describes the part of the landscape in which these dogs were originally employed – having been bred to drive badgers, foxes, rabbits, and other quarry from their underground retreats. On occasions, when the terrier could not reach into the burrow or earth, it would still indicate the presence of the quarry to the hunter, who would then unearth it by other means.

Because of the qualities required to perform these underground tasks, most terriers are small to medium-sized dogs, often with short legs, great digging skills and powerful jaws – but always with huge amounts of courage and tenacity. In time, the name terrier came to be applied to all dogs that were also kept for despatching vermin such as rats and mice. Because different sorts of terriers were required for working over many varied kinds of terrain, cross-breeding with

A West Highland White Terrier.

other types of dogs became common practice. Thus breeds of terrier required to keep up with huntsmen on horseback might be bred with hounds to improve the stamina and increase the length of the legs. Terriers used for fighting would be bred with mastiffs and other large, powerful dogs to improve their skills in combat. Many of these new terrier breeds arose because of local needs, and often bear the name of the region in which they originated. The West Highland White Terrier, the Irish Terrier, and the Scottish Terrier, for example, leave no doubt as to their origins.

Terriers range in size from the largest, the Airedale Terrier (which is 24 inches/61cm at the shoulder), to the much smaller Norfolk Terrier (which stands only 10 inches/25.5cm high). Despite these great differences in size, terriers usually display many shared characteristics. They are naturally alert and curious dogs, being sharp in movement, and their ancestry means that they like nothing better than to explore underground at any opportunity. They also have a great propensity for digging – much to the alarm and consternation of owners with well-kept gardens.

On the whole, terriers are robust dogs, and less sensitive than many other pedigree breeds. For this reason, they make good pets for a young growing family.

AIREDALE TERRIER

This breed, the largest by far of all the terriers (and sometimes called the King of Terriers for this reason), originated in Yorkshire, England. The dog reflects both terrier and hound ancestry in its makeup and behavior, although it is too big to go underground in the traditional way of terriers. The Airedale Terrier's imposing size means that it is used on occasions as a guard dog, among other duties.

A muscular, cobby, and active-looking dog, the head is long and flat and not too broad between the ears, and the nose is black. The dark eyes should have a lively expression. The V-shaped ears are small, folded and placed high at the sides of the head. The neck is muscular and is carried on a body with a short, strong and level back; the chest is deep. The legs are long and well-boned. The tail is strong and carried high; it is customarily docked.

The texture of the coat is hard, wiry, and dense; undercoat is softer. Color is tan, with black or grizzle saddle, top of neck and top of tail.

The dog's remarkable scenting powers mean that it is used for tracking, for detecting victims in collapsed buildings, and for game hunting. The Airedale also comes into its own as an intelligent and courageous guard dog. Nevertheless, the breed makes a devoted and protective family dog

Size *Height:* dog 23–24in (58.5–61cm); bitch 22–23in (56–58.5cm).
Weight: 45lb (20.5kg).

The Airedale is known for its excellent sense of smell and tracking

BEDLINGTON TERRIER

A dog with one of the longest traceable pedigrees of any terrier, the Bedlington hails from Rothbury in north-east England – indeed, its original name was the Rothbury Terrier. The high-arched back suggests some Whippet blood in its ancestry, among other breeds.

A graceful and muscular dog with a large, wedge-shaped head. The skull is narrow, deep, and rounded. The eyes are small, bright, and triangular; colors vary with the coat color. The ears are moderately long and hang flat to the cheeks. The neck is long and tapering and is carried on a long, muscular body with a deep chest and arched back and loins. The legs are moderately long and end in hare-feet. The tail is long and tapering, and is never held over the back.

The coat is thick and with a characteristic texture described as 'linty,' and with a tendency to twist on the head and face. Usually trimmed to produce the appearance so distinctive of the breed. Colors are blue, blue-and-tan, liver or, sandy.

The gentle and unusual appearance of this dog belies its true terrier nature. It is capable of fast movement, when its characteristic mincing gait can be seen during slower speeds.

Size *Height:* 16in (41cm). *Weight:* 18–23lb (8–10.5kg).

BORDER TERRIER

The Border Terrier comes from the border region between England and Scotland, although the name is probably a reference to the fact that the dog worked with the Border Foxhounds. A true worker, the dog was bred to enter fox lairs to flush out the occupants and also needed to be able to keep up with riders on horseback.

The head is shaped like that of an otter but with a broad skull and a short, strong muzzle. The nose is black, liver, or flesh-colored. The dark eyes have an alert expression. The ears are small, V-shaped and folded. The strong neck

is carried on a deep, narrow, and fairly long body. The legs are moderately long. The tail is fairly short and carried high, although not over the back.

The coat is thick and harsh with a dense undercoat. Colors are red, wheaten, tan-and-grizzle, or tan-and-blue.

This dog is as it looks; a strong, well-boned and active little terrier whose job is to go to ground to flush out foxes. Its legs are sufficiently long for it to keep up with riders on horseback, yet the dog is small enough to pick up when necessary.

Size *Height:* dog 12in (30.5cm); bitch 11in (28cm). *Weight:* dog 13–15.5lb (6–7kg); bitch 11–14lb (5–6.5kg).

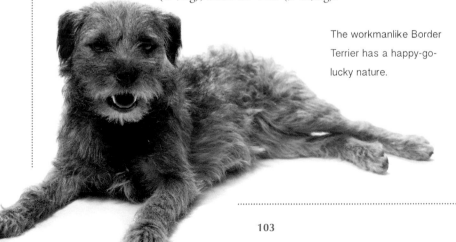

The workmanlike Border Terrier has a happy-go-lucky nature.

103

BULL TERRIER

The Bull Terrier was first bred in Birmingham, England, by crossing dogs with Bulldog and terrier blood with English White Terriers. A miniature Bull Terrier also exists; this is almost identical in appearance to the standard Bull Terrier, but is only 14 inches (35.5cm) in height.

A muscular, stocky dog with a characteristic egg-shaped head. The long, strong head has powerful jaws and a gently sloping profile from the top of the head down to the nose tip. The nose is black. The eyes are narrow, triangular, and slanting. The ears are small and pricked. The neck is long and muscular. The body has a very broad chest when viewed from the front and a short, strong back. The legs are moderately long with strong bones. The tail is short and carried horizontally.

The coat is short, flat, and harsh but with a gloss. Colors are either pure white or black, brindle, fawn, red, or tricolor.

Despite this dog's rather intimidating appearance – it stands four-square in a manner not unlike a bull, from which its name is partly derived – it is in fact well-disposed towards human beings, although it needs firm handling to ensure a peaceful coexistence with other dogs.

Size *Height:* 18in (46cm). *Weight:* 72lb (33kg).

CAIRN TERRIER

The Highlands of Scotland and the Isle of Skye are the original home of the Cairn Terrier, where it was bred for hunting otters, badgers, and foxes. No longer required for these duties, the breed nevertheless remains a popular dog for the house.

A game little dog with a wiry, slightly unkempt look. The head is small with a broad skull and a powerful muzzle. The nose is black. The hazel eyes are deep-set and offset by shaggy eyebrows. The small, pointed ears are pricked. The compact body is strong, with a deep chest and a level back. The legs are short and strongly-boned. The tail is short and well-covered with hair.

The Cairn is a delightful and fun-loving dog and needs only moderate exercise.

THE FAITHFUL DOG

The Cairn has a thick, harsh outercoat with a short, close undercoat. Colors are cream, red, wheaten, gray, or nearly black – all of these colors may be brindled. The ears and muzzle may be darker.

An alert and endearingly mischievous-looking dog, the Cairn Terrier is fearless and ready for anything.

Size *Height:* 11–12in
(28–30.5cm).
Weight: 14–16lb
(6–7.5kg).

SMOOTH FOX TERRIER

This is one of the most popular and well-established of all terriers. It originated in Britain and has an ancestry that is probably linked with Bull Terriers and Manchester Terriers. This terrier is a valuable addition to the foxhound pack, being small enough to chase foxes from cover which is too inaccessible to be reached by larger dogs.

A compact and purposeful-looking dog, the skull is flat and rather narrow, and the muzzle is long and strong. The nose is black. The eyes are small and dark with an alert, intelligent expression. The breed has small, V-shaped drop ears. The neck is moderately long, lean, and muscular. The body has a deep chest and a short, level back. The legs are quite long and strong. The tail is docked and carried jauntily.

The coat is smooth, short, hard, and dense. Preferred colors are all-white, black-and-white, or tan-and-white.

Big enough to cope with foxes and strong enough to run with a hunt, the Smooth Fox Terrier is lively and eager. The breed needs a firm hand but rewards a caring owner with devotion and affection.

Size *Height:* dog 15.5in (39.5cm); bitch proportionately smaller. *Weight:* dog 16–18lb (7–8kg); bitch 15–17lb (7–7.5kg).

WIRE FOX TERRIER

It is likely that the Wire Fox Terrier was developed before its smooth-haired counterpart, although it was the latter that appeared first in the show ring. The Wire Fox Terrier was originally called the Rough-haired Terrier. A popular family dog, the breed appears at its best when trimmed into the classic shape.

A compact and well-balanced dog, the skull is flat, rather narrow, and slightly sloping. The muzzle is long and strong, and the nose is black. The eyes are small and dark with an alert, intelligent expression. The small drop ears are V-shaped and moderately thick. The neck is fairly long, lean and muscular. The body has a deep chest and

The energetic Wire Fox Terrier will expect to be included in every game.

a short, level back. The legs are strong and muscular. The tail is docked and carried erect.

The coat is wiry and dense with an undercoat of shorter, softer hair. Color is mainly white with black, tan, or black-and-tan markings.

Bred for sporting pursuits, this is another big-hearted terrier. Fearless and ever-ready, the breed also makes an excellent family pet, expecting to join in every game and ever on guard in case of intruders.

Size *Height:* dog 15.5in (39.5cm); bitch proportionately smaller.
Weight: dog 16–18lb (7–8kg); bitch 15–17lb (7–7.5kg).

"Every dog has its day."

IRISH TERRIER

The Irish Terrier, or Irish Red Terrier as it was once called, was first shown in Ireland in the 1870s, although it had been used by sportsmen for many years before that – and indeed still is. This was the first Irish dog breed to be recognized by the Kennel Club.

A wiry, racy-looking dog with an attractive reddish coat. The head is long with a flat, fairly narrow skull. The nose is black. The eyes are dark and lively. The drop ears are small and V-shaped. The neck is of fair length and is carried by a moderately-long body with a straight, strong back; the loins are muscular and slightly arched. The legs are quite long with plenty of muscle and bone. The tail is usually docked to about three-quarters of its length.

The Irish Terrier enjoys family life, and given a firm hand makes an affectionate pet.

The coat is hard and wiry, with a broken appearance. Colors are red, red-wheaten, or yellow-and-red.

The breed has a reputation for being a bit of a daredevil – rushing into action without fear of the consequences. It can also be intolerant of other dogs. But with its human companions it is the very model of devotion, sensitivity, affection, and good nature.

Size *Height*: dog 19in (48cm); bitch 18in (46cm). *Weight*: dog 27lb (12kg); bitch 25lb (11.5kg).

"The dog is a gentleman; I hope to go to his heaven, not man's."

Mark Twain (1835–1910)

113

KERRY BLUE TERRIER

The Kerry Blue Terrier is believed to have originated in Kerry, Ireland, where it was used, originally by farmers, for hunting foxes, otters and badgers. Nowadays, however, with careful trimming to achieve the classic Kerry shape, it has been transformed into a successful show dog.

A well-proportioned, muscular and upstanding dog, the long, lean head has strong, deep jaws and a fairly long muzzle. The nose is black. The eyes are small and dark and have a typically keen terrier expression. The V-shaped, drop ears are small. The neck is long and is carried on a short, deep-chested body. The

The Kerry shape must be carefully maintained if you decide to show it.

legs are long and powerful and end in small feet. The tail, customarily docked, is carried erect.

The coat is profuse, soft, and wavy. The color may be any shade of blue. Puppies are born black, and the color may take up to 18 months to develop.

This is an extrovert and determined dog, bred for an outdoor life. It shows many of the characteristics typical of terriers. Bold and game, the breed also makes a good pet and house guard. Regular trimming is required to maintain the typical 'look.'

Size *Height:* dog 18–19in (46–48cm); bitch slightly less. *Weight:* dog 33–37lb (15–17kg); bitch 35lb (16kg)

LAKELAND TERRIER

The Lakeland Terrier was developed in the Lake District of England, its role being to run with the fox hunts. Regular grooming is needed to maintain the dog's classic appearance.

An attractive, compact, and purposeful-looking dog. The head features a flat skull and a broad, moderately-long muzzle. The nose is black, except in liver-colored dogs when the nose is also liver. The eyes are hazel or a darker shade. The ears are V-shaped and folded. The neck is slightly arched and carried on a shortish body with a strong back. The legs are long and powerful. The tail is customarily docked and carried high but never over the back.

The coat is dense, hard, and weatherproof. Colors are black-and-tan, blue-and-tan, wheaten, red, red-gray, liver, blue, or black.

Although small, the Lakeland Terrier is a tough, fearless and active dog, ever-alert and ready to work all day if necessary. This breed is so endearingly cheerful and affectionate that even its sometimes naughty ways are soon forgiven.

Size *Height:* 14.5in (37cm). *Weight:* dog 17lb (7.5kg); bitch 15lb (7kg).

MINIATURE SCHNAUZER

This bright and lively German dog is believed to have originated through crossing a Schnauzer with the Affenpinscher. The Miniature Schnauzer has very much of the terrier in its appearance and character – and indeed, in America, it is placed within that group. Schnauzers come in two other sizes in addition to the one described here.

A sturdy, alert-looking dog of nearly square proportions. The head is long with a flat skull and strong muzzle. The nose is black. The dark eyes are oval and set forward in the skull. The V-shaped ears are usually folded forward,

although in some countries they are cropped. The arched, moderately-long neck is carried on a short body with a fairly deep chest. The legs are well-boned and muscular. The tail is usually docked.

The coat is rough and wiry, with a bushy beard and eyebrows. Colors are pure black, black-and-silver, or all pepper-and-salt (dark gray) colors and white.

Alert and quick-moving, the Miniature Schnauzer makes the ideal companion – whether it be for an active family, looking for a dog to join in the fun, or an older person needing a trusted and loyal friend.

Size *Height:* dog 14in (35.5cm); bitch 13in (33cm). *Weight:* dog 20lb (9kg); bitch 16.5lb (7.5kg).

The Miniature Schnauzer is a sturdy, well-proportioned little dog.

NORFOLK TERRIER & NORWICH TERRIER

The Norfolk Terrier, and the almost identical Norwich Terrier, take their names from the English county (in the case of the Norfolk) and city (in the case of the Norwich). The breeds came about by crossing small red terriers with other terriers. Originally, there was no distinction between the Norfolk and the Norwich, but in 1964 it was decided that dogs with drop ears would be called Norfolk Terriers and dogs with prick ears would be classed as Norwich Terriers. The descriptions which follow apply to both breeds, with the exception of the style of ears already described.

A small, compact, and keen-looking dog. The head has a broad, slightly-rounded skull. The muzzle is wedge-shaped with a well-defined stop. The oval eyes are deep-set and either black or dark-brown; they should have a keen and alert expression. The ears are medium-sized and pointed; in the Norfolk Terrier they are folded, and in the Norwich Terrier the ears are erect. A strong, medium-length neck is carried on a short, compact body. The legs are shortish but strong. The tail may be docked, but this is optional.

The coat is hard, straight, and wiry and is slightly longer on the neck and shoulders; hair on head and ears is shorter and smoother. Colors are red, wheaten, grizzle, or black-and-tan.

These tough, active little dogs love to dig and to explore any holes large enough to enter. Thoroughly fearless, they make lovable, friendly pets.

Size *Height:* 10in (25.5cm).
Weight: 10–12lb (4.5–5.5kg).

The Norfolk Terrier is the drop-eared version of the Norwich Terrier, which is prick-eared.

PARSON RUSSELL TERRIER
(Parson Jack Russell)

The Parson Russell Terrier gets its name from a Devonshire parson, the Reverend Jack Russell, who was a keen huntsman who bred a small, active terrier using, among others, Fox Terriers. The dog has now achieved show status and comes in either smooth-coated or rough-coated forms. The Parson Russell described here is a longer-legged animal than the short-legged Jack Russell Terrier so commonly seen in farmyards and family homes.

A no-nonsense dog resembling a shorter-legged Fox Terrier. The head has a moderately broad and flat skull, the nose is black. Keen, almond-shaped eyes give the dog an alert expression. The ears are V-shaped and folded. The neck is medium-length and muscular and is carried on a body with a strong, straight back. The legs are strong and muscular. The tail is straight, and is usually docked.

Hard, dense, and close in both smooth-coated and rough-coated varieties. Colors are all-white, or white with tan, lemon, or black markings.

A tough, active little worker, bred for pace and endurance. A playful and intelligent rascal with sharp eyes and wits to match, the Parson Jack Russell makes a good house pet.

Size *Height:* dog 13–14in (33–35.5cm);
bitch 13in (33cm).
Weight: 14lb (6.5kg).

The Parson Russell Terrier may be small but on occasions can be willful.

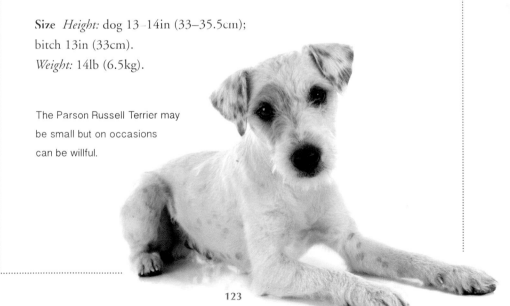

SCOTTISH TERRIER

A breed which hails from the Highlands of Scotland, the dog was originally used to destroy rodents and foxes. The standard for the breed was drawn up in 1880, and the Scottish Terrier Club was formed in 1882. Although still fairly popular, the Scottish Terrier is less commonly seen than it was about 50 years ago.

A sturdy, short-legged and thick-set dog, the head gives the impression of being large in comparison with the body size. The head is long with a flat skull. The dark-brown eyes are deeply set beneath long eyebrows. The ears are finely pointed and pricked. A muscular neck is carried on a body with a deep chest and a short, muscular back. Short, strong legs terminate in good-sized feet. The tail is of moderate length and tapers at the tip.

The outercoat is hard, dense, and wiry, and the undercoat is short, soft, and dense. Colors are black, wheaten, or brindle.

Somewhat reserved at times, the 'Scottie' is a vigilant and loyal companion. When ready for a game, the Scottish Terrier can move remarkably swiftly in pursuit of a toy such as a ball.

Size *Height:* 10–11in (25.5–28cm). *Weight:* 19–23lb (8.5–10.5kg).

The Scottish Terrier is capable of a good burst of speed when the mood takes it. It is also an excellent watchdog.

SOFT COATED WHEATEN TERRIER

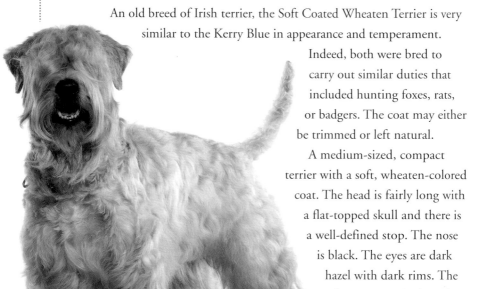

An old breed of Irish terrier, the Soft Coated Wheaten Terrier is very similar to the Kerry Blue in appearance and temperament. Indeed, both were bred to carry out similar duties that included hunting foxes, rats, or badgers. The coat may either be trimmed or left natural.

A medium-sized, compact terrier with a soft, wheaten-colored coat. The head is fairly long with a flat-topped skull and there is a well-defined stop. The nose is black. The eyes are dark hazel with dark rims. The drop ears are V-shaped.

The neck is moderately-long, arched, and muscular. A short and compact body is carried on strong, moderately-long legs. The tail, customarily docked, is carried jauntily but never arched over the back.

The coat is soft and silky; curled or loosely waved. The coat is especially profuse on the head and legs. Color should be clearly wheaten.

A natural sort of terrier with an extrovert and playful disposition, the Soft Coated Wheaten is ready for action at any time.

Size *Height:* dog 18–19.5in (46–49.5cm); bitch slightly less. *Weight:* dog 35–45lb (16–20.5kg); bitch slightly less.

The Soft Coated Wheaten Terrier is now rare in Ireland from where it is thought to have originated.

STAFFORDSHIRE BULL TERRIER

The result of crossings between Bulldog and terrier, the Staffordshire Bull Terrier was bred and used as a fighting dog until this cruel pastime was abolished. The name 'Staffordshire' comes from the breed's association with the Black Country area of England where it originated.

A smooth-coated dog of muscular build and with a low center of gravity, the head is short and deep with a broad skull and prominent cheek muscles. The nose is black. The round, medium-sized eyes are usually of a dark color, but this may vary according to coat tone. The ears are rose or half-pricked. A short, muscular neck is carried on a body with a broad chest and strong shoulders. The legs are well-boned and set wide apart. The tail is of medium length and carried rather low.

The coat is short, smooth, and close-lying. Colors are red, fawn, white, black, or blue, or any of these colors with white; also brindle or brindle-and-white.

The breed's reputation as a pugnacious fighter means that it needs careful training and firm handling when near other dogs. With humans, however, the Staffordshire Bull Terrier is affectionate and calm.

Size *Height:* 14–16in (35.5–40.5cm).
Weight: dog 28–38lb (13–17kg); bitch 24–34lb (11–15kg).

With firm control and careful training, the Staffordshire Bull Terrier makes a loving family pet.

WEST HIGHLAND WHITE TERRIER

The breed is thought to have originated in Poltallock, Scotland, where the Malcolm family bred these white terriers for several generations. In fact, the dogs were originally called Poltallock Terriers. These smart little sporting dogs are also much admired in the show ring and as companions.

An eager, squarely-built little terrier with a characteristic white coat, the head has a slightly arched skull with a tapering muzzle and a black nose. The medium-sized eyes are set wide apart; their color should be as dark as possible and should impart a keen expression. The ears are

The West Highland White Terrier has a cheeky little face and will never refuse the opportunity for a game.

small, erect, and pointed. The body is compact, with a deep chest and broad, strong loins. The legs are short and strong. The tail should be as straight as possible and is carried jauntily.

The outercoat is harsh, long, and free from curl; undercoat is short, soft, and close. Color should be pure white.

The 'Westie' is a deservedly popular little dog. Possessing a lively and outgoing personality, the dog is always ready for a game and seems to be full of boundless energy. A sharp bark to warn off strangers also makes it a useful guard dog.

Size *Height:* 11in (28cm).
Weight: dog 19lb (8.5kg);
bitch 16.5lb (7.5kg).

THE NON-SPORTING GROUP

The non-sporting group is a classification of dogs that are appreciated first and foremost for their companionship qualities but which may also undertake other useful roles such as guarding property. But all of the breeds found within the non-sporting group do seem to have an hereditary aptitude for defending and guarding. Some, like the Bulldog, were originally bred as fighting dogs, and these aggressive qualities have stood them in good stead when required to stand guard. This is a virtue no less important today than in the past, for it is a well-known fact that a property guarded by a loudly barking dog is a much less attractive proposition for a would-be burglar than one in

A Boston Terrier.

OPPOSITE: A beautiful Standard Poodle.

which the arrival of a stranger is greeted with silence. Although the modern-day non-sporting dog is not usually pugnacious by nature, most will be prepared to respond appropriately if there is a real threat to the family or home that they think they are guarding.

Among the diverse shapes and sizes to be found within the non-sporting group, there is one group of dogs that is fairly uniform in type and appearance. These are the spitz breeds, which are of Arctic origin, and these hardy animals were bred to work in the harsh and inhospitable conditions of the frozen north. Spitz dogs were, and in some places still are, expected to carry out a wide range of tasks. These include guarding duties for domestic herds, working as

The Dalmatian is a very athletic dog and is a keen runner.

OPPOSITE: Cheerful and friendly, the German Spitz enjoys joining in all the family games.

watchdogs, hunting, and acting as draft dogs – pulling sleds or carrying tents and other equipment on their backs. They probably also served a useful function by being something warm to sleep next to at night.

Some of the other dogs within the non-sporting group can also be trained to perform useful tasks over and above those of guard or companion. The Dalmatian, a keen and powerful runner, can be trained for hunting and retrieving. Poodles, too, have considerable retrieving skills and are particularly adept at gathering from the water. Poodles are also sometimes used to sniff out valuable truffles from below the ground.

"The dog wags his tail, not for you,
but for your bread."

Portuguese Proverb

BICHON FRISE

This sprightly little dog originated in the Mediterranean region, possibly as long ago as the 14th century, but later found favor in the royal courts of Europe. After the French Revolution, the dog became a familiar part of circus acts, but by the 19th century its popularity had declined. The breed's fortunes, however, were restored when it was recognized by the French Kennel Club in 1934.

A sturdy, lively little dog with a thick woolly coat, the head has a broad skull with a shortish muzzle. The nose is black. The eyes are large, dark, and round and face forward prominently; their expression is one of alertness. The ears are pendulous. An arched, moderately-long neck is carried on a

body with a well-developed chest and broad loins. The legs are straight and well-boned. The tail is usually carried in a curve over the back.

The coat is thick, silky, and loosely curled and often clipped into a distinctive shape. The color should be solid white.

Lively and confident, the Bichon Frise is happiest when receiving plenty of attention from its owners. It likes to join in family games and is undemanding both in terms of diet and exercise.

Size *Height:* 9–11in (23–28cm).
Weight: 6.5–13lb (3–6kg).

The Bichon Frise is an enchanting and undemanding pet. It enjoys partaking in family activities.

BOSTON TERRIER

The ancestors of this American breed include Bulldogs and Bull Terriers. Derived from pit fighting dogs, the first of the breed appeared in the 1890s around Boston. The animal is striking to look at, and is often regarded as the national dog of America. In America, and to a lesser extent in Britain, it is a popular show dog and companion.

A muscular dog with distinctive, erect ears, and a striking coat, the head is square-shaped with a short, wide muzzle. The nose is black. The large, round eyes are set wide apart and have an alert expression. The ears are carried erect. The slightly arched neck is carried on a short, deep-chested

The Boston Terrier is an attractive little dog and one of the most popular American breeds.

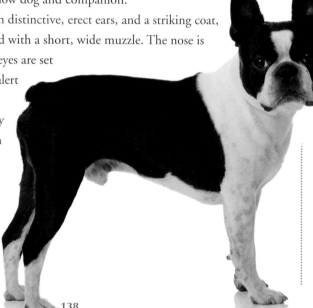

138

body. The legs are strong and muscular. The tail is short and tapering; it may be straight or screw.

Short and glossy. Brindle-and-white are the preferred colors, but black-and-white is also permissible.

A dapper-looking, small to medium-sized dog, the Boston Terrier is quite strong-willed and determined, but nevertheless makes an amiable and intelligent house dog.

Size *Height:* 15–17in (38–43cm). *Weight:* Not to exceed 25lb (11.5kg). Divided into 3 classes as follows: under 15lb (7kg); 15–20lb (7–9kg); and 20–25lb (9–11.5kg).

BULLDOG

The Bulldog is the national dog of Britain and is known the world over as a symbol of indomitable spirit and determination. The history of the Bulldog probably goes back to at least the 1600s, when it was used for bull-baiting and dog fights. Fortunately this was abolished in the 19th century when the Bulldog became a show dog and companion.

A massively-built, low-slung, sturdy dog, the head is imposing and deep with a broad, square skull and a short, broad muzzle with an upturned lower jaw. The nose is black. The eyes are round, set wide apart, and have a quizzical, appealing expression. The rose ears are small. The neck is very thick, deep and powerful. The body is short, broad in front and narrow towards the rear; the chest is

The Bulldog has a reliable temperament and its protective nature makes it a good watchdog.

140

deep and broad. The fore legs are stout and placed so far apart that they appear to be slightly bowed, although the bones themselves are actually straight; the hind legs arc longer. The tail is rather short and tapers to a fine point.

The coat is fine, close, and short. Colors are whole or smut (in other words, whole color with a black muzzle or mask), brindles, reds plus shades such as fawn, white, and pied (in other words, white with any of the aforementioned colors).

The Bulldog's pugilistic appearance belies an affectionate nature. Somewhat stubborn and tenacious on occasions, the breed is nevertheless good with children and makes a protective watchdog when required.

Size *Height:* 12–14in (30.5–36cm). *Weight:* dog 55lb (25kg); bitch 50lb (22.5kg).

CHINESE SHAR-PEI

A Chinese breed, the Shar-Pei was originally bred for use as a guard, hunter and herding dog. This is a most unusual-looking dog, with a suggestion of Mastiff in its ancestry.

A squarely-built dog with a characteristically wrinkled skin and frowning expression. The head is rather large and rectangular, and the muzzle is long, broad, and padded. The nose is preferably black, but any color harmonizing with the coat color is allowed. The eyes are almond-shaped and may be dark or light, depending on the coat color. The ears are small, triangular, and folded. The neck is short and strong. The body is short and deep and slightly raised under the loins.

The Chinese Shar-Pei has an unusual look which is not to everyone's taste, it has nevertheless many enthusiastic fans.

The legs are muscular and strong. The tail tapers at the tip and may be carried high and curved or curled over the back.

The coat is bristly, short, and hard and standing off from the body. Colors are solid black, red, cream, or fawn.

This is a vigorous and active dog. Early exports were reported to have had some problems with their temperament, but the breed has improved over the last ten to 15 years.

Size *Height:* 18–20in (46–51cm). *Weight:* 35–44lb (16–20kg).

CHOW CHOW

The Chow Chow is a spitz-type dog that has been known in China for about 2,000 years. In China, the dog was used as a guard, a companion, and for hunting. There are two versions of the Chow Chow: a smooth-coated variety and a rough-coated variety.

A heavy-looking, woolly-coated dog with a lion-like appearance. The head has a heavy, broad skull and a medium-length, broad muzzle. The nose is black. The gums, roof of the mouth and tongue are blue-black. The eyes are dark and oval-shaped. The ears are small and pricked. A strong neck is carried on a short, broad, deep-chested body. The legs are heavily-boned and muscular. The tail is carried curled over the back.

Rough-coated dogs have a coat which is thick and abundant; the

outercoat is somewhat coarse and the undercoat is soft and woolly; it is especially thick around the neck and behind the legs. In smooth-coated dogs the coat is short, dense, straight, and plush. Colors are solid black, red, blue, cream, fawn, or white.

The Chow Chow does not take readily to strangers, although it is loyal towards its owner.

Size *Height:* dog 19–22in (48–56cm); bitch 18–20in (46–51cm). *Weight:* 55lb (25kg).

DALMATIAN

Another breed that is recognizable by almost anyone with a passing interest in dogs, the Dalmatian was highly popular in Britain during the Regency period. Then it was also known as the 'carriage dog,' since it used to run alongside, or even underneath, all kinds of carriages. Today, the Dalmatian is a popular, friendly, and long-lived pet.

A clean-looking, elegant, and athletic dog with a distinctive coat pattern. The head is fairly long, with a broad skull and a long, strong muzzle. The nose is black in black-spotted varieties and brown in liver-spotted

The Dalmation has abundant energy and is a rewarding pet for owners who have time to exercise and train it.

146

individuals. The eyes are dark or amber, according to the coat color; they should look bright and express intelligence. The ears are fairly large and pendulous. A long, well-arched neck is carried on a deep-chested body with a powerful back. The legs are long and muscular. The tail is long and carried with a slight upward curve when on the move.

The coat is short, dense, glossy, and sleek. The ground color is pure white, evenly covered with either black or liver spots.

The Dalmatian has great freedom of movement, using a long-striding, rhythmic action. A good sporting dog if required – with boundless energy and enthusiasm.

Size *Height:* dog 23–24in (58.5–61cm); bitch 22–23in (56–58.5cm). *Weight:* dog 55lb (25kg); bitch 49.5lb (22kg).

"The more I see of men, the more I like dogs."

Germaine de Staël (1766–1817)

GERMAN SPITZ

In Germany, there are five different varieties of spitz dogs, ranging in size from the large Wolfspitz to the small Pomeranian. The two varieties described here are the *klein* (small) and the *mittel* (medium) varieties. Apart from the difference in size, they are identical.

A compact, full-coated dog with erect ears. The head has a broad, flattish skull with the muzzle narrowing to a wedge. The nose is either black or a color harmonizing with the coat color. The eyes are dark; either black or a tone harmonizing with the coat color. The small ears are held completely erect. The body is short, with well-developed loins. The legs are well-boned and terminate in cat-feet. The tail is curled and held up over the back.

The coat is double consisting of a long, hard, straight outercoat and a soft, woolly undercoat. The fur is very thick around the neck and forequarters. All colors are acceptable, including chocolate, white, and fawn.

Cheerful and friendly with an undemanding appetite, the German Spitz enjoys joining in all the family games. Its long coat will keep it warm in the coldest weather, but requires thorough grooming to look its best.

Size *Height:* small 9–11.5in (23–29cm); medium 12–15in (30–38cm). *Weight:* small 17.5–22lb (8–10kg); medium 23–25lb (10.5–11.5kg).

The German Spitz makes a fine pet and has a cheerful personality. However, it will require careful grooming to enhance its beautiful coat.

POODLE

The Poodle, one of the most well-known breeds, comes in three sizes: Toy, Miniature, and Standard. It is also one of the most recognizable of breeds, due mainly to the fact that its fur is often clipped into a very distinctive shape. Although considered to be a French dog, it is more likely that the breed actually originated in Germany and was later taken to France. In the United States the Toy Poodle is placed in the toy group.

An elegant and balanced dog with a distinctive coat, the head is long with a moderately-broad skull and a strong muzzle. The almond-shaped eyes are black or dark-brown, and express intelligence and vivacity. The ears are long and hang close to the face. The

neck is strong and carries the head with dignity. The body is broad and deep-chested, with powerful loins. The legs are long and well-boned. The tail is usually docked and is carried away from the body at a slight angle.

The coat is dense and profuse with a harsh texture and does not molt; it is often given a lion clip or the less fussy Dutch clip. All solid colors are permitted.

Poodles are intelligent dogs, once highly prized as performing animals for circuses and stage shows due to their ability to learn quickly. The two smaller breeds are the most suited to a life in town, whereas the Standard is a real country dog at heart.

Size *Height:* Miniature 11–15in (28–38cm); Standard over 15in (38cm). *Weight:* Miniature 13lb (6kg); Standard 66–75lb (30–34kg).

OPPOSITE: A handsome Standard Poodle.

A Miniature Poodle.

151

TIBETAN TERRIER

The Tibetan Terrier has a history going back over 2,000 years, and in its native lands the breed was thought to bring luck to its owner as well as having religious associations. Although they are called terriers, they are in fact herding dogs.

A well-built, long-coated dog reminiscent of a small Old English Sheepdog. The head has a medium-length skull and a strong muzzle. The nose is black. The round, dark-brown eyes are large and set wide apart. The V-shaped ears are pendent and heavily feathered.

The neck is of medium length and is carried on a compact and well-muscled body. The legs are well-boned and terminate in large, round feet. The well-plumed tail is carried curled over the back.

The outercoat is profuse, fine, and long and may be straight or waved, but not curled; the undercoat is fine and woolly. Colors are white, cream, golden, smoke, gray, black, parti-color, or tricolor.

This is the largest of the Tibetan breeds in the group. An energetic and enthusiastic dog, the Tibetan Terrier is friendly to those it knows, loyal and bursting with character.

Size *Height:* dog 14–16in (35.5–40.5cm); bitch slightly smaller. *Weight:* 18–31lb (8–14kg).

The Tibetian Terrier is bursting with energy, and requires regular play sessions to maintain its zest for life.

THE HERDING GROUP

The herding dog was born when man came down from the mountains and began to settle in the fertile valleys and lowlands. They no longer needed the large and often cumbersome dogs to guard them, such as the Pyrenean Mountain Dog, and the requirement now was for smaller, faster, and more mobile dogs that could keep large flocks of domestic animals together. New breeds were developed, such as the various types of collies and the quick-moving Australian Cattle Dog.

Some of the world's working sheepdogs are hardly ever seen outside their native countries, and the qualities that suited them for a life spent working with livestock do not always translate into suitable attributes for the show ring or even family life.

The qualities required of a herding dog include the ability to control large flocks of cattle, sheep, goats, or other livestock and to quickly and obediently respond to the commands of the shepherd. It is also vital that the dogs are instinctively protective towards their owner and the animals in their care.

These traits, together with a high degree of intelligence and willingness to be trained, mean that dogs of this type also make excellent guard dogs. Herding dogs tend to be energetic, highly intelligent, and good-natured. They also have an enormous amount of surplus energy and require a good deal of exercise to keep then fit in mind and body.

OPPOSITE: The Pyrenean Mountain Dog is an old breed that is more suited to guarding than herding.

The Australian Cattle Dog is a fast, agile, and intelligent breed used for herding.

155

AUSTRALIAN CATTLE DOG

A tough breed, developed to control cattle on the long journeys to market, the Australian Cattle Dog is also known by other names, including the Blue Heeler and the Australian Heeler – 'Heeler' being a reference to the dog's habit of nipping the heels of cattle when maneuvering them. The breed was developed initially by crossings involving sheepdogs, the Dingo, the Kelpie, the Dalmatian, and the Bulldog.

A compact, tough, and symmetrical-looking dog with a typical sheep-herder's head. The head is wedge-shaped with a broad skull and a medium-length muzzle. The nose is black. The brown eyes are alert and intelligent. The ears are broad at the base, pricked, and pointed. The neck is very strong and muscular. The body has a deep, broad chest and is carried on strong legs. The tail resembles a fox's.

The outercoat is hard, straight and weather-resistant; undercoat is short and dense. Colors are blue, blue-mottled or blue-speckled with tan, blue or black markings; or red-speckled with red markings.

Watchful and intelligent, the Australian Cattle Dog loves to work. It is tireless and capable of fast movements.

Size *Height:* dog 18–20in (46–51cm); bitch 17–19in (43–48cm). *Weight:* 35–44lb (16–20kg).

AUSTRALIAN SHEPHERD

Despite its name, the Australian Shepherd did not in fact originate in Australia. Its roots lie in the sheepdogs of the Basque region of Spain, and when Basque shepherds emigrated to Australia with their herds in the 19th century they took some of their dogs with them. Later, these people and their dogs moved again, this time to America, where the dogs finally got their name.

A long-bodied, well-balanced dog. The head has a squarish and slightly domed skull and the muzzle is slightly tapering towards the nose. The nose is variously colored; it is black in blacks and blue merles and liver or brown in reds and red merles. The oval-shaped, moderately-sized eyes are blue, amber or brown, odd-colored, or a combination with flecks and marbling. The triangular ears are set high on the head. The neck is of moderate length and is carried on a strong, deep-chested body with a level back. The legs are of medium length. The tail is straight and may be docked.

The coat is straight or wavy and of medium length and texture; the undercoat is weatherproof. Colors are black, blue merle, red, or red merle; all of these colors may have tan points.

An agile, sure-footed dog with well-developed herding and guarding instincts. The Australian Shepherd Dog is nevertheless friendly – although sometimes reserved initially – and quick and eager to learn.

Size *Height:* dog 20–23in (51–58.5cm); bitch 18–21in (46–53.5cm).
Weight: 35–70.5lb (16–32kg).

BEARDED COLLIE

It is possible that the origins of the Bearded Collie go back to the 16th century, when Polish Lowland Sheepdogs, brought to Scotland by visiting sailors, were bred with local herding dogs. Today, the Bearded Collie is one of the most popular and instantly recognizable of all dog breeds.

A long-coated, lean, and active dog, the head has a broad, flat skull, and a fairly long muzzle. The nose is usually black, but may be of a color harmonizing with the coat in blues or browns. The eyes also harmonize with the coat color, and should be large,

expressive and friendly. The ears are moderately large and hang down. The slightly arched neck is carried on a deep-chested body with strong loins. The legs are well-boned and muscular. The long tail is normally carried low, with a slight upward curl at the end, but extends when on the move.

The outercoat is flat, strong, and shaggy; the undercoat is soft and close; the coat should be long enough to enhance the shape of the dog and to form the characteristic beard. Colors are slate-gray, reddish-fawn, black, all shades of gray, brown, and sand, with or without white markings.

An active, self-confident, and fun-loving dog with an endearing expression, the Bearded Collie is many people's idea of the perfect pet – although it also makes a highly capable working dog.

Size *Height:* dog 21–22in (53.5–56cm); bitch 20–21in (51–53.5cm).
Weight: 39.5–59.5lb (18–27kg).

The Bearded Collie needs daily grooming to keep matting and molting hairs at bay, but most think the extra care is well worth the trouble.

BELGIAN SHEPHERD DOG

The Belgian Shepherd Dog has a history stretching back to the Middle Ages, but in the 1890s the breed was differentiated into three separate coat types and four coat-color patterns. The basic body shape of each of these types remains the same, however. Each of the four types of Belgian Shepherd is named after a region in Belgium. These are the Groenendael, the Tervueren, the Malinois, and the Laekenois. All of these dogs are sheepdogs and guards, but they are increasingly seen as pet dogs, too.

A medium to large, well-balanced and square dog, carrying itself elegantly and proudly; some types are slightly reminiscent of the German Shepherd. The head is fairly long, the skull and muzzle being almost equal in length; the muzzle tapers towards the nose, which is black. The brown eyes are almond-shaped, of medium size and present a direct, quizzical expression. The ears are triangular, stiff and erect. The neck is well-muscled and broad at the shoulders. The body is deep-chested and powerful; the rump slopes slightly. The legs are well-boned and muscular. The tail is long.

Coat types and coat-color patterns are as follows:

Groenendael: Outercoat long, straight and abundant and fairly harsh; undercoat dense; hair particularly long around neck forming a ruff; fringe of long hair on back of fore legs; hair also long on

OPPOSITE: A Groenendael.

Pictured left is a wiry coated Laekenois and right is a Tervueren.

tail and hindquarters; hair longer on dogs than on bitches. Color is black, or black with small amounts of white on chest and parts of feet.

Tervueren: Coat similar to that of the Groenendael in length and texture. Colors are red, fawn, or gray, with black tipping – this feature especially apparent on shoulders, back, and ribs.

Malinois: Coat thick and close; undercoat woolly; hair especially short on head, ears and lower legs; short on rest of body but thicker on tail and around neck; fringing on parts of legs. Colors are similar to those of the Tervueren.

Laekenois: Coat is hard and wiry but not actually curled; about 2.5in (6-5cm) in length. Color is reddish-fawn with black shading, especially on the muzzle and tail.

An intelligent and alert breed that is also graceful and dignified. Loyal and obedient, the Belgian Shepherd is protective of its owner and property. These dogs require plenty of exercise.

Size *Height:* dog 24–26in (61–66cm); bitch 22–24in (56–61cm). *Weight:* 60.5–63lb (27.5–28.5kg).

OPPOSITE: A Malinois Belgian Shepherd.

BORDER COLLIE

Recognized the world over as one of the finest and most intelligent of all sheepdogs, the Border Collie was formerly used in the border regions between England, Scotland, and Wales, but is now found far and wide. A graceful, balanced dog with a low-slung body. The head has a fairly broad skull and a shortish, straight muzzle tapering to the nose. The nose is usually black but may be brown, chocolate, or slate to harmonize with other coat colors. The oval eyes are brown, but in merles one or both

The Border Collie is an active dog with boundless energy and consequently requires plenty of exercise.

may be blue; the eyes have an alert and intelligent expression. The ears are medium-sized and are carried semi-erect or erect. The strong, slightly-arched neck is carried on a long, athletic-looking body with a deep chest. The medium-length legs are strong and muscular. The tail is moderately long and raised when on the move, but never carried over the back.

Moderately-long; the outercoat is dense and medium-textured, and the undercoat is soft and dense. Various colors are possible, including black, black-and-white, and tan-and-white.

Keen, alert, responsive, hard-working, and intelligent – these are some of the qualities that have made the Border Collie such a successful farm dog. The breed is also loyal and faithful and responds well to commands.

Size *Height:* dog 21in (53.5cm); bitch 20in (51cm).
Weight: dog 52lb (23.5kg); bitch 42lb (19kg).

167

ROUGH COLLIE

Basically the same breed as the Smooth Collie, the Rough Collie evolved from the dark-coated herding dogs of Scotland. These in turn may have had their origins when dogs brought to Scotland by the Romans were mated with local dogs. The Rough Collie achieved royal recognition when Queen Victoria kept the breed at Balmoral Castle in Scotland. Although this form of the breed is today more likely to be seen in the show ring than working on the hills with sheep, it nevertheless retains many of its herding instincts.

An attractively-coated, well-proportioned dog, the wedge-shaped head has a flat and fairly wide skull and a long muzzle. The nose is black. The eyes are medium-sized and almond-shaped and

The Rough Collie or "Lassie" dog has been popular as a pet for a good many years.

have a gentle expression; the color is dark-brown, except in blue merle-coated dogs when they are blue or blue-flecked. The ears are held back when resting, but when the dog is alert they are brought forward and held semi-erect. The neck is powerful and arched, and is carried on a rather long body with a deep chest. The legs are strongly-boned and terminate in oval feet. The long tail is held low at rest but raised when on the move, although never over the back.

The coat is very dense, with the outercoat straight and harsh; the undercoat soft and close; the mane and frill very abundant. Colors are sable-and-white, tricolor, or blue merle; all colors also include white.

This elegant and beautifully-coated dog makes an ideal pet, being friendly and loyal, especially towards its owner. The coat needs plenty of grooming to retain its luxurious condition.

Size *Height:* dog 22–24in (56–61cm); bitch 20–22in (51–56cm). *Weight:* dog 45–65lb (20.5–29.5kg); bitch 40–55lb (18–25kg).

"*The dog's kennel is not the place to keep a sausage.*"
Danish proverb

SMOOTH COLLIE

This breed is essentially a short-coated version of the Rough Collie, and also comes from Scotland. The same color varieties are available. Many consider this breed to be the more attractive and practical of the two.

A dog of dignified appearance, giving the impression of ability in the field. The wedge-shaped head has a flat and fairly wide skull and a long muzzle. The nose is black. The eyes are medium-sized and almond-shaped and should have a gentle expression; the color is dark-brown, except in blue merle-coated dogs when they are blue or blue-flecked. The ears are held back when resting, but when the dog is alert they are brought forward and held semi-erect. The neck is powerful and arched, and is carried on a rather long body with a

170

deep chest. The legs are strongly-boned and terminate in oval feet. The long tail is held low at rest but raised when on the move, although never over the back.

The outercoat is short, flat, and harsh; the undercoat is dense. Colors are sable-and-white, tricolor, or blue merle; all colors may also include white.

This elegant dog makes an ideal pet, being friendly and loyal especially towards its owner. More of a working dog than its close relative, the Rough Collie, this breed expects rather more exercise.

Size *Height:* dog 22–24in (56–61cm); bitch 20–22in (51–56cm). *Weight:* dog 45–65lb (20.5–29.5kg); bitch 40–55lb (18–25kg).

The Smooth Collie is a handsome workdog. it makes a loyal and friendly pet that requires plenty of exercise.

171

GERMAN SHEPHERD DOG

One of the most popular and instantly recognizable dogs anywhere, the German Shepherd is a byword for excellence and versatility throughout the canine world. Bred to the standard we know today in the later part of the 19th century by German army officer Max von Stephanitz, the breed was originally used as a sheep-herding dog. Later, however, it found favor as a police and military dog.

An alert, long-bodied, purposeful-looking dog. The head has a moderately-broad skull and a long muzzle. The eyes are almond-shaped, usually brown, and should convey intelligence and confidence. The ears are medium-sized, broad at the base, and carried erect. The neck is long, strong and muscular. The deep-chested body is long with a straight back that slopes towards the hindquarters; the body-length

The German Shepherd requires an experienced handler. The long-coated variety is very beautiful but not always accepted for show purposes.

should be slightly greater than the dog's height. The legs are strong and muscular. The tail is long and bushy and hangs in a curve at rest.

The outercoat is close, straight, hard, and weather-resistant; the undercoat thick, woolly, and close. Colors include black, black-and-tan, and sable; occasionally white or cream dogs appear.

A good-quality German Shepherd Dog will make a highly trainable, tireless, intelligent and loyal companion.

Size *Height:* dog 25in (63.5cm); bitch 23in (58.5cm).
Weight: dog 80.5lb (36.5kg); bitch 65lb (29.5kg).

OLD ENGLISH SHEEPDOG

Another of the almost universally recognized breeds of dog, the Old English Sheepdog, or Bobtail as it is also known, probably evolved through crossings between European sheepdogs and British sheepdogs over 150 years ago. The breed's coat is its most distinctive feature – indeed, there is little else of the actual dog to be seen unless the coat has been clipped.

A strong, symmetrical, square dog, the head also has a rather square skull and a strong, square muzzle. The nose is black. The eyes may be dark or wall-eyed; sometimes the eyes are blue. The ears are small and carried close to the sides of the head. The neck is fairly long and arched. The short, compact body with muscular loins is carried on long, strongly-boned legs. The tail is usually completely docked.

Hard-textured and profuse, the coat should be free from curl but shaggy; the undercoat should be waterproof. Colors are gray, grizzle, or blue in any shade; the head, neck, forequarters, and under-belly should be white, with or without markings.

Cheerful and extroverted, the Old English Sheepdog is always ready to join in any activity. The breed needs plenty of exercise, and careful, regular grooming is required to avoid the coat from becoming hopelessly matted and tangled.

Size *Height:* dog 24in (61cm) minimum; bitch 22in (56cm) minimum.
Weight: dog 80.5lb (36.5kg); bitch 65lb (29.5kg).

"Let Hercules himself do what he may,
The cat will mew and dog will have
his day."

William Shakespeare (1564–1616)

Having been bred for hard work, the Old English Sheepdog needs a good deal of exercise.

175

POLISH LOWLAND SHEEPDOG

With an ancestry that is believed to include the Hungarian Puli and long-coated herding dogs, the Polish Lowland Sheepdog has been in existence since the 16th century at least. Polish sailors visiting British seaports in the 16th century are thought to have exchanged these dogs for native ones, and so helped the breed to spread.

A chunky, muscular, long-coated breed reminiscent of the Bearded Collie, the head has a fairly broad, slightly arched skull with a muzzle equal in length to the skull. The nose should be as dark as possible. The eyes are hazel or brown and have an alert expression. The moderately large drop ears are heart-shaped. The neck is muscular and strong.

The body is rectangular in side view with a level back and muscular loins and is carried on well-muscled legs. The tail is usually docked, although some dogs are born tailless.

The coat is long, thick, and shaggy with a hard texture; the undercoat is soft; the eyes are covered by long hair. Any colors are acceptable.

This is a lively, intelligent and friendly dog that seems particularly fond of playing with children. The Polish Lowland Sheepdog needs plenty of exercise.

Size *Height:* dog 17–20in (43–51cm); bitch 16–18.5in (40.5–47cm). *Weight:* 43lb (19.5kg).

The Polish Lowland Sheepdog is full of energy and exuberance. It requires plenty of exercise and regular grooming.

PYRENEAN MOUNTAIN DOG

For centuries, this large and impressive dog was used to guard flocks against wolves, bears, and other predators in the Pyrenees of France. A descendant of the herding and guard breeds of southern Europe, the breed was a favorite with French noblemen.

Strong, well-balanced, and elegant, the head has a broad, fairly-arched skull and a medium-length, slightly-tapering muzzle. The nose is black. The almond-shaped eyes have a thoughtful expression and are dark amber in color. The ears are triangular and lie at the sides of the head when the dog is resting. The neck is thick and muscular. The chest is broad and deep and the back is broad and muscular. The legs are heavily-boned and well-muscled, as befits such a

The Pyrenean Mountain Dog was originally used to protect flocks of sheep against wolves. It is now mainly used as a pet.

powerful dog; the double dew-claws help the dog to tackle the mountainous terrain. The tail tapers towards the tip and is carried with the tip slightly curled.

The outercoat is fairly long, coarse, and thick; it may be straight or wavy; the undercoat is profuse; the coat forms a mane around neck and shoulders. Colors are white, or white with patches of badger, wolf-gray, or pale-yellow.

The Pyrenean Mountain Dog has a confident, kindly, and dignified air about it, although, like any big dog, it needs proper handling.

Size *Height:* dog 28in (71cm) minimum; bitch 26in (66cm) minimum. *Weight:* dog 110lb (50kg) minimum; bitch 90lb (41kg) minimum.

SHETLAND SHEEPDOG

The bleak Shetland Islands, off the north-east coast of Scotland, are the original home of this small dog, which bears a strong resemblance to the Rough Collie. Although small, the breed was quite capable of working with the smaller Shetland ponies and other livestock of the area.

An elegant and symmetrical sheepdog, the head is in the shape of a blunt wedge, with a flat, fairly broad skull, and a long, rounded muzzle. The nose is black. The almond-shaped eyes are obliquely set and are usually dark-brown, although they may be blue or blue-flecked in merles. The small ears are usually carried semi-

The Sheltie has brains as well as beauty and, like the Shetland pony, has been miniaturized, in this case, from the Collie.

erect with the tips falling forward. The well-arched neck is carried on a deep-chested body with a level back. The muscular legs are moderately long. The tail is well-furred.

The outercoat of long hair is hard and straight; the undercoat is soft and short; hair forms an abundant mane and frill. Colors are sable, tricolor, blue merle, black-and-white, and black-and-tan.

This attractive little dog makes a good companion for people of all ages, being watchful, intelligent, and active.

Size *Height:* dog 14.5in (37cm); bitch 14in (35.5cm). *Weight:* 20lb (9kg).

"A dog owns nothing, yet is seldom dissatisfied.."
Irish proverb

WELSH CORGI (CARDIGAN)

Originally bred as a cattle dog, the Cardigan Welsh Corgi is the older of the two varieties of Welsh Corgi, with a history going back 800 years. Nevertheless, it is the least well-known of the two breeds. It is also the only one with a tail, and the Cardigan differs from the Pembroke in other respects, too, such as in coat-color, ear-length, and foot-shape.

A sturdy, short-legged, and active dog, the head has a fox-like shape with a wide, flat skull, and a tapering muzzle. The nose is black. The eyes have an alert but kindly expression and should be dark, although one or both may be blue or blue-flecked in merles. The ears are proportionately large with rounded tips, wide-spaced, and held erect. A muscular neck is carried on a long, fairly broad-chested body. The legs are short but strong, and the feet are round. The brush-like tail is long enough to touch the ground but is usually lifted when on the move.

The coat is weatherproof; short or slightly longer, and with a hard texture. Any colors are permitted.

Active and fast-moving on occasions, the Cardigan Welsh Corgi can also take life at a steadier pace when it feels like it. Intelligent and obedient, the breed makes a good companion and watchdog.

Size *Height:* 12in (30.5cm). *Weight:* 22–24lb (10–11kg).

WELSH CORGI (PEMBROKE)

The better-known of the two breeds of Welsh Corgi, this version usually has its tail docked. Another cattle-driving dog, the Pembroke also earned its keep by nipping at the heels of cattle to encourage them to move on – a trick that has been tried on humans on occasions as well! This breed also has a long working history, as well as being the favorite pet of Queen Elizabeth II of England, who has owned many examples of this dog over the years.

A sturdy, short-legged, and active dog, the head has a fox-like shape with a wide, flat skull and a tapering muzzle. The nose is black. The round eyes are brown in

The Pembroke Corgi's chief claim to fame is its popularity with the British Royal Family, since the Queen has kept Corgis for many years.

color. The ears are of medium size with rounded tips, wide-spaced and held erect. A fairly long, muscular neck is carried on a long, fairly broad-chested body. The legs are short but strong, and the feet are oval. The tail is usually docked.

The coat is weatherproof; short or slightly longer and with a hard texture. Colors are red, sable, fawn, or black-and-tan, usually with white markings on the legs, neck, chest, and face.

A popular and outgoing dog, the Pembroke makes a good companion for an active family. It likes nothing more than a good romp out in the open air, followed by a square meal. Its fondness for food should be moderated, however, to avoid obesity.

Size *Height:* 10–12in (25.5–30.5cm). *Weight:* 22–24lb (10–11kg).

THE WORKING GROUP

The working group features breeds that, between them, do a variety of work – guarding, carrying loads, or pulling sleds and other vehicles, law enforcement duties, and rescue work, for example. Some are bred to carry out more than one task. Thus, for example, the Alaskan Malamute is a powerful sled-pulling dog, but its huge size and loud bark mean that it also performs an important role as a guard dog. In addition to these roles, many of the dogs in this group are among the most popular of pets.

The working dog has within its group animals of hugely differing shapes and dimensions. They range in size from the small German Pinscher, standing only 17–19 inches (43–48cm) high, to the giant of the group – the Anatolian Shepherd Dog at 32 inches (81cm). Although this huge dog is the tallest of the group, it is not the heaviest; the Mastiff can weigh up to 190lb (86kg). Despite any differences in vital statistics, what these dogs all have in common is generation upon generation of breeding that has brought them to the peak of perfection. Each dog, whatever its size, is ideally suited to the task expected of it. Many are indispensable servants of mankind. Most also share common traits of intelligence and obedience and an inbuilt desire to do the job for which they were bred.

Nomadic shepherd tribes adopted mountain dogs to act as guards, both to protect the herd from marauding wolves, bears, and other predators, and to act as watchdogs against thieves and other enemies of the tribesmen. Thus the dogs had to be big, strong, and courageous. Interestingly, light-colored or even white dogs were

OPPOSITE: The Anatolian Shepherd Dog originates in Turkey where it was highly prized for guarding flocks.

The Alaskan Malamute has huge amounts of energy and stamina.

favored, since at night they could be more easily distinguished from attackers by the shepherds.

Later, as some of these mountain tribes began to settle in the fertile valleys and lowlands, the need for such large and often cumbersome dogs began to diminish. The requirement now was for smaller, faster and more mobile dogs that could keep large flocks of domestic animals together. Many of these dogs became the ancestors of modern-day sheepdogs, such as the various types of collies, as well as the quick-moving Australian Cattle Dog. *See section: The Herding Group.*

It is also vital that the dogs are instinctively protective towards their owner and the animals they are looking after. These traits, together with a high degree of intelligence and willingness to be trained, mean that dogs of this type also make excellent guard dogs. This is not to say that training is always a simple task, however. Many of these breeds are strong-minded – and strong-bodied – dogs that need some initial convincing that their owner's bidding is the best course of action for them!

The working dogs whose role was primarily to guard property and people are the Boxer, the Bullmastiff, and the Dobermann. These are all strong, active dogs with highly developed protective instincts. Although this

quality is one of their main virtues, it must not be allowed to develop to the extent that the dog becomes overprotective and aggressive. Difficult behavior in such large and potentially dangerous dogs can be a real problem, and ownership of such breeds must be considered carefully and correct training and handling adhered to at all times. It is vital that dogs such as these are fully aware of their place in the 'pack' and respond quickly and consistently to commands from their owner.

The Dobermann has a highly protective nature. However, with early and careful traning they can make good pets.

AKITA

Also known as the Akita Inu, meaning 'large dog,' the Akita is Japan's largest and best-known breed. Its origins can be traced back to the polar regions, from where spitz-type dogs reached northern Japan. Originally used for fighting, as well as for hunting bears and wild boar, the breed is mainly used today as a guard and army dog.

An immensely powerful and striking dog with a bear-like face. The head has a fairly broad skull and a medium-length, strong muzzle. The nose is black. The small, almond-shaped eyes are brown. The hooded ears are fairly small, triangular, and set wide apart; they are held firmly erect. A thick, muscular neck is carried on a body with a deep, wide chest and a level back.

The Akita is brave and affectionate but has a will to dominate at times. This dog requires firm controlling.

190

The legs are well-boned, strong, and muscular. The tail is large, and carried curled over the back.

A double coat consisting of a coarse, straight outercoat and a soft undercoat. The coat may be of any color, such as white, brindle, or gray, but should be brilliant and clean; a contrasting mask is often present.

The Japanese Akita is reserved and protective but clearly likes to dominate; the dog requires firm controlling by its owner to remind it who is in charge.

Size *Height:* dog 26–28in (66–71cm); bitch 24–26in (61–66cm).
Weight: 110lb (50kg).

ALASKAN MALAMUTE

This large dog of Alaskan origin is named after a local Inuit tribe. The Alaskan Malamute was bred for pulling sleds for long distances over the frozen terrain of Alaska and northern Canada. In fact, it is the largest of all the sled dogs.

A powerfully-built, handsome dog, the head is broad, with a skull that narrows towards the eyes. The muzzle is large and the nose is usually black, although in red-and-white examples it is brown. The almond-shaped eyes are usually brown; darker shades are preferred, except in red-and-white dogs when the eyes may be lighter. The

The Alaskan Malamute is a strong working dog with great stamina for pulling sleds.

ears are small and triangular and are normally held erect but may also be held close to the skull. The strong neck is carried on a deep-chested and powerfully-built body with strong loins. The legs are well-muscled and strong. The tail may hang down at rest but is usually carried curled loosely over the back when working.

The Malamute has a thick, coarse, outercoat and dense, oily and woolly undercoat. Colors range from solid white, gray through to black, and from gold through red shades to liver; the underbody, legs, feet and mask are always white.

Although this strong dog is not especially fast, it needs plenty of exercise and has the power to pull enormous weights for long distances – therefore it can also take some stopping if it has a mind to carry on.

Size Height: dog 25–28in (63.5–71cm); bitch 23–26in (58.5–66cm).
Weight: 85–125lb (38.5–56.5kg).

BERNESE MOUNTAIN DOG

It is likely that the foundations for this large, affable dog arose from crossings of local Swiss herding dogs and a type of guard dog brought by invading Roman armies into what is now Switzerland about 2,000 years ago. The dog gets its name from the Swiss canton of Bern.

A stocky, well-balanced dog with an attractive coat, the head has a broad skull and a medium-sized muzzle. The almond-shaped eyes are dark-brown and convey a kindly expression. The ears are medium-sized and triangular. A strong and muscular neck is carried on a compact body with a deep chest and a strong, level back. The legs are strongly-boned and well-muscled. The bushy tail is held raised when on the move.

Long, soft and silky; a slight wave is allowed, but the coat should not be curly. The color is jet black with russet-brown or tan markings; a white blaze is present on the head and a white cross on the chest; white paws and a white tail-tip are desirable.

A delightful and well-mannered character, full of good humor and responsive to training. It makes the perfect companion for a country-dwelling owner.

Size *Height:* dog 25–27.5in (63.5–70cm); bitch 23–26in (58.5–66cm). *Weight:* 87–90lb (39.5–41kg).

BOXER

The likely ancestors of the Boxer are the Bulldog and the Great Dane. A German breed, the Boxer has existed in the form seen today for over 100 years. The breed became unpopular during the First World War, but its popularity was later restored – no doubt due mainly to its virtues as a guard dog and active companion.

Clean and hard in appearance, the Boxer is a squarely-built and active dog. The head is short and square, with the skin forming wrinkles. The muzzle is broad and deep, with the lower jaw undershot and curving slightly upward. The nose is black. The dark-brown eyes face well forward and wear a lively and alert expression. The ears are set wide apart at the top of the skull and lie flat to the cheeks when resting, but fall forward when alert; ears may be cropped and erect in some countries. The neck is round and

The Boxer needs firm handling and an energetic owner. Once correctly trained, it makes a loyal and faithful pet as well as a good watchdog.

196

strong. The body is short and deep-chested with a strong, slightly-sloping, straight back. The muscular legs are moderately long and terminate in cat-feet. The tail is usually docked.

The coat is short, hard, and glossy. Colors are shades of fawn or brindle with white.

An extrovert by nature, the Boxer is fearless and confident. Although loyal to family and friends, it can be wary of strangers and therefore makes an efficient guard dog.

Size *Height:* dog 25–27.5in (63.5–70cm); bitch 23–26in (58.5–66cm).
Weight: 87–90lb (39.5–41kg).

> "I have a dog of Blenheim birth,
> With fine long ears and full of mirth;
> And sometimes, running o'er the plain,
> He tumbles on his nose:
> But quickly jumping up again,
> Like lightning on he goes!"
>
> John Ruskin (1819–1900)

197

BULLMASTIFF

The Bullmastiff came about through crossings between the Bulldog and the Old English Mastiff. The dog was used as a very effective guard dog and gamekeeper's dog – in fact, it was often known as 'the gamekeeper's dog.'

A powerful and symmetrical dog with a smooth coat. The head has a square skull and a deep, strong muzzle. The skin on the head becomes wrinkled when the dog is aroused. The eyes are hazel or darker in color and of medium size. Ears are V-shaped and folded, and help to accentuate the impression of squareness of the skull. The neck is very muscular and almost as wide as the skull. The body is short with a broad chest and a straight back and carried on moderate-length, powerful legs. The tail is long and tapering.

The coat short and hard, lying flat to the body. Colors may be any shade of brindle, fawn, or red.

A powerful and purposeful dog with an independent nature, the Bullmastiff is not recommended for the novice dog owner. However, it is reliable, faithful, and affectionate, and makes an excellent guard dog.

Size *Height:* dog 25–27in (63.5–68.5cm); bitch 24–26in (61–66cm).
Weight: dog 110–130lb (50–59kg); bitch 90–110lb (41–50kg).

DOBERMANN PINSCHER

The breed takes its name from Louis Dobermann, a German tax collector who bred the dog in the 1870s. He crossed a variety of dogs, including German Shepherd, Pinscher, Rottweiler, and Manchester Terrier to produce an animal capable of protecting him – and also of encouraging recalcitrant debtors to pay up! Given its pedigree, it is not surprising that the Dobermann Pinscher reflects many virtues, including speed, strength, and intelligence.

Muscular and elegant, with a smooth, glossy coat, the head has a fairly narrow, flat skull with a rather long, deep muzzle. The nose is solid black in black dogs, dark-brown in brown dogs, dark-gray in blue individual dogs, and light-brown in fawn dogs. The eyes are fairly deep-set and should convey a lively

The Dobermann Pinscher is an elegant breed, combining a muscular frame with a glossy short coat.

and intelligent expression. The neat ears may be erect or dropped; in some countries they are docked. A long and lean neck is carried on a deep-chested body with a short, firm back. The legs are long and well-boned and terminate in cat-feet. The tail is usually docked.

The coat is smooth, short, and close-lying. Colors are black, blue, brown, or fawn, with tan markings above the eyes, on the muzzle, throat, chest, legs, feet, and tail.

The Dobermann Pinscher can make a highly intelligent, loyal, and delightful pet for owners willing to train it carefully from puppyhood and be firm and consistent in handling the dog, so that it knows who is in charge.

Size *Height:* dog 27in (68.5cm); bitch 25.5in (65cm).
Weight: dog 83lb (37.5kg); bitch 73lb (33kg).

GIANT SCHNAUZER

This is the biggest of the three Schnauzer breeds, used in Bavaria in Germany as long ago as the 15th century for herding duties. It started to become redundant in this role when railways became a more economical option for moving cattle about. But the Giant Schnauzer's impressive size and appearance meant that it soon found favor in the cities of Germany as a guard dog.

A powerful, long-legged, and almost square dog, the head has a fairly broad skull and a long, strong muzzle. The nose is black. The eyes are oval and dark. The V-shaped ears drop forward to the temple. The strong neck is slightly arched and is carried on a body with a broad, deep chest, and a strong, straight back. The legs are long and well-boned. The tail is customarily docked.

The outercoat is hard and wiry, and there should be a good

202

undercoat; there are prominent beard, moustache, and eyebrows. Colors are pure-black or pepper-and-salt.

Intelligent, strong, and active, the Giant Schnauzer is also friendly and reliable. Its size and boldness mean that it can also act as a very effective deterrent to a would-be burglar.

Size *Height:* dog 25.5–27.5in (65–70cm); bitch 23.5–25.5in (60–65cm). *Weight:* dog 100lb (45.5kg); bitch 90lb (41kg).

The Giant Schnauzer is a powerful dog with an amiable personality and makes an imposing guard dog.

GREAT DANE

Despite its name, the Great Dane is of German origin and not Danish. In fact, it has been the national dog of Germany since 1876. Originally used to hunt wild boar, the breed was initially classed as a hound, and it undoubtedly has hound blood – possibly Greyhound – in its makeup.

Muscular, elegant, and of imposing appearance, the head has a flattish skull and a deep, broad muzzle. The eyes are round, medium-sized, and dark in color; in harlequins odd or wall eyes are permissible. The ears are triangular and folded forward; in some countries, such as America, the ears are docked. The neck is long and arched, and held well up. The body is deep, with slightly-arched loins. The legs are long and muscular and terminate in cat-feet. The long tail tapers towards the tip.

The coat is short, dense, and glossy. Colors are brindles, fawns, blues, black, or harlequin (pure white background with black patches or blue patches appearing ragged).

A majestic-looking dog with a dignified and friendly nature, the Great Dane is only suitable for those with the space to house this huge dog and the budget to keep up with its appetite.

Size *Height:* dog 30in (76cm); bitch 28in (71cm) – these are minimum height requirements. *Weight:* dog 119lb (54kg); bitch 101.5lb (46kg).

MASTIFF

This huge breed is one of the oldest in Britain, and dogs similar in appearance to the modern Mastiff were to be found at the time of the Roman invasion of Britain, fighting alongside their masters as they tried to repel the invaders.

A massive, powerfully-built dog with a large, heavily-jowled head. The head has a square skull, a short, broad muzzle, and a marked stop. The small eyes are set wide apart, are brown in color and give an impression of calmness and strength. The ears are small and thin and hang down by the sides of the head. The neck is highly muscular. The body has a deep, wide chest, and a very muscular back and loins. The legs are large-boned and muscular. The tail tapers at the tip and is held slightly curved when the dog is on the move.

The coat is short. Colors are apricot-fawn, silver-fawn, fawn, or fawn brindle, and black brindle.

Fortunately, this large and impressive dog is docile and good-natured, but it still makes an admirable guard dog. It is affectionate and loyal and needs plenty of human company and reasonable amounts of exercise.

Size *Height:* 27.5–30in (70–76cm). *Weight:* 174–190lb (79–86kg).

Despite its imposing size, the Mastiff is a quiet and docile animal and thrives on human company and regular exercise. They are known for their voracious appetites.

NEWFOUNDLAND

The exact origins of the Newfoundland are somewhat obscure, but it is possible that the breed developed from a type of dog that was brought by nomadic peoples into the northern polar regions and not actually from Newfoundland itself. From there, the breed was taken by sailors and traders to England, where it became very popular.

A big-boned, strong-looking dog, the head is broad and massive with a short, square muzzle. The dark-brown eyes are small and deep set. The ears are also small and fall close to the sides of the head. A strong neck is carried on a deep-chested body with muscular loins. The legs are of moderate length and strongly boned, terminating in webbed feet – an invaluable aid to swimming. The tail is of medium length.

Oily, waterproof, and double; the coat is flat and dense. Colors are black, brown (chocolate or

bronze), or landseer – this last color, named after the painter Sir Edwin Landseer who illustrated the breed on many occasions, is white with black markings.

When one thinks of dogs and water, the name Newfoundland invariably springs to mind. No other breed has such a natural affinity with water. Used for centuries to help fishermen retrieve their nets, the Newfoundland also has a deserved reputation as a powerful swimmer and life-saver.

Size *Height:* dog 28in (71cm); bitch 26in (66cm). *Weight:* dog 140–150lb (63.5–68kg); bitch 110–120lb (50–54.5kg).

The Newfoundland is a powerful swimmer and is renowned for its life-saving capability. For centuries they have been used as fishermen's companions.

PORTUGUESE WATER DOG

This dog probably arrived in Portugal with Moorish traders from North Africa. For centuries, the breed's great love of water has been put to good use by Portuguese fishermen who use the dog for salvaging tackle and nets from the water and for guarding the boats. Webbed feet help the dog to swim. The dog comes in two different coat types – a long, wavy coat and a shorter, curly coat.

A rectangular, muscular dog reminiscent of a Poodle, the head has a long skull and a strong, slightly-tapering muzzle. The eyes are round and are dark-brown or black in color. The drop ears are heart-shaped. The neck is short and straight and is carried on a short, deep-chested body. The long legs are well-boned and muscular and end in webbed feet. The tail is long and tapering and is carried in a ring-shaped arch over the back; a plume of hair is left on the end.

The Portuguese Water Dog has two distinctive coat types; *Long-coated:* Thick and loosely waved; fairly glossy. *Short-coated:* Harsh and dense with tight curls; not glossy. Coat clipped into characteristic style. Colors are black, white, brown, black-and-white, or brown-and-white.

The Portuguese Water Dog is cheerful, intelligent, and energetic, with excellent swimming ability.

Size *Height:* dog 19.5–22.5in (49.5–57cm); bitch 17–20.5in (43–52cm). *Weight:* dog 42–55lb (19–25kg); bitch 35–48lb (16–22kg).

As the name suggests, the Portuguese Water Dog loves water and has webbed feet.

ROTTWEILER

The name of this dog comes from the Roman settlement of Rottweil in Germany. When the Roman Empire was invading Germany, mastiff-type dogs were brought along too, for guarding and herding livestock. In time, Rottweil became an important trading center for cattle and other livestock, and butchers in the town used the dog for various duties, including pulling carts.

A compact, powerful, and well-proportioned dog, the head has a wide, medium-length skull, and a deep, broad muzzle. The nose is black. The brown eyes are almond-shaped. The ears are small and pendent. The neck is strong, round, and very muscular. The body has a broad, deep chest with a straight, strong back. The legs are well-boned and muscular. The tail is normally docked at the first joint.

The outercoat is of medium-length, coarse and flat; the undercoat should not be visible through the outercoat. Color is black with well-defined tan markings on cheeks, muzzle, chest, legs, over the eyes, and under the tail.

Bold, loyal, and courageous, the Rottweiler is also an active dog that likes plenty of exercise. This is a willing worker and an excellent guard dog, but firm handling and training are essential for ownership of such a strong dog.

Size *Height:* dog 25–27in (63.5–68.5cm); bitch 23–25in (58.5–63.5cm). *Weight:* dog 110lb (50kg); bitch 85lb (38.5kg).

The Rottweiler is a formidable animal and requires careful handling from puppyhood to make it manageable. Not for the faint-hearted.

SAINT BERNARD

It would be difficult to mistake the St Bernard for any other dog, for this gentle giant is depicted everywhere as a symbol of rescue and care. A descendant of mastiff-type dogs brought to the Swiss Alps by the Romans over 2,000 years ago, the dog achieved fame when it was used by the monks at the Hospice of St Bernard for rescuing travelers lost in the St Gothard Pass. The dog comes in two coat varieties, a rough-coated form and a smooth-coated form.

A well-proportioned, massive dog of substance. The huge head has a broad, slightly-rounded skull and a short, deep muzzle. The nose is black. The dark eyes are medium-sized and should have a benevolent expression. The triangular ears are medium-sized and lie close to the cheeks. The neck is thick and muscular with a well-developed dewlap. The deep-chested body has a straight back and muscular loins and is carried on straight, heavy-boned legs. The feet are large, which no doubt help the dog to progress through snow. The tail is long.

The St Bernard has two distinctive coat types; *Rough-coated:* Flat and dense and full around the neck. *Smooth-coated:* Close-fitting and hound-like with feathering on the thighs and tail. Colors are orange, mahogany-brindle, red-brindle, or white with patches on the body of any of these colors.

Fortunately, this massive dog has an extremely benevolent temperament and a steady, calm nature. Walks are usually taken at a leisurely pace, but a St Bernard can pull extremely hard, so it needs to be under control.

Size *Height:* dog 28in (71cm) minimum; bitch 26in (66cm) minimum. *Weight:* dog 165.5lb (75kg); bitch 150lb (68kg).

The St Bernard has a placid, affectionate nature, but because of its massive size and strength requires careful training. Remember, also, that it has a very large appetite.

SAMOYED

The Samoyed was originally used to guard the reindeer herds and pull the sleds of the wandering tribesmen of the Siberian tundra. Fur traders brought the breed back to Britain.

A well-proportioned, graceful, spitz-type dog with a sparkling, stand-off coat. The head is wedge-shaped with a wide skull and a medium-length muzzle. The nose may be black, brown, or flesh-colored. The brown eyes are almond-shaped and enhance the 'laughing' expression so characteristic of this dog. The ears are thick with slightly rounded tips, and are held erect. The strong neck is carried on a broad, muscular body with a deep chest. The legs are very muscular and well-boned. The tail is held curled over the back and to one side.

The Samoyed has a thick, close, short undercoat and a harsh, straight outercoat which grows away from the body to give protection from the cold. Colors are pure white, white-and-biscuit, and cream.

The Samoyed is a charming dog that loves human company. Fairly obedient in a rather laid-back way, the breed nevertheless enjoys life and lets everyone know it.

Size *Height:* dog 20 22in (51–56cm); bitch 18–20in (46–51cm). *Weight:* dog 50.5lb (23kg); bitch 39.5lb (18kg).

The Samoyed makes an excellent family pet. It is a lively, jolly animal and fairly obedient, having a mind of its own. However, its thick coat can be rather troublesome in hot weather and requires regular grooming.

SIBERIAN HUSKY

The Siberian Husky was developed by the Chukchi peoples of Arctic north-east Asia as a fast, long-distance sled dog. Indeed, this is the fastest of all the sled-pulling breeds, and the dog seems happiest when performing this task.

A purposeful, medium-sized sled dog, the head is rather fox-like in shape, with a slightly rounded skull and a medium-length muzzle. The nose is black in gray, black or tan dogs, liver in copper-colored dogs, and flesh-colored in white individuals. The eyes are almond-shaped and may be brown or blue, or parti-colored. The triangular ears are held firmly erect. The neck is arched and is carried on a medium-length, muscular and deep-chested body. Well-muscled, powerful legs end in oval, slightly webbed feet with fur between the toes. The tail has a fox-like brush.

The outercoat is straight and smooth-lying; undercoat soft and dense. The coat may be of any color, including white.

Friendly and extremely tolerant towards humans, the same cannot always be said about the Siberian Husky's attitude to other dogs, which it will usually try to dominate. Indifferent to the coldest of weather, the breed is not a typical pet by any means. The breed is mostly kept for sled racing.

Size *Height:* dog 21–23in (53.5–58.5cm); bitch 20–22in (51–56cm). *Weight:* dog 45–60lb (20.5–27kg); bitch 35–50lb (16–22.5kg).

The Siberian Husky, having been bred for harsher climates and to pull heavy loads, is not the ideal pet. It can also be aggressive to other dogs and because of its dense coat is not very happy indoors.

THE TOY GROUP

Some groups – the hounds, the gundogs and the terrier group, for instance – are made up of dogs sharing common characteristics. Within each of these groups, therefore, we find dogs with either an inbuilt tendency to hunt or to retrieve or to go to earth in pursuit of quarry. The toy group also includes dogs that have one overriding characteristic in common. In this case, it is that they are all small – even if they come in a variety of different shapes. In this respect, therefore, the toy group shares a common link with the aforementioned groups, yet it also has similarities with the working dog group and the non-sporting dog group, both of which also have a heterogeneous collection of breeds within them.

The dogs in the toy group are bred with a different purpose in mind, too. Although many breeds within the other groups are kept solely as pets, their original purpose is to perform some kind of work or other. Toy dogs are bred primarily to be companions (although many of them also make excellent watchdogs and some can catch vermin very adequately).

Despite their small size, toy dogs are still dogs, and they should be treated as such. They may not need to expend as much energy as some other breeds, but they still need adequate amounts of exercise and a proper canine diet. Being carried around all day and fed sweets and other inappropriate food is a demeaning way to treat a dog. Given the chance, most toy breeds will enjoy a romp in the open air and can normally give a good account of themselves when confronted by larger varieties of their species. A properly treated dog, whatever its size, will repay the kindness shown to it with affection and by being an amusing and stimulating companion. Most toy breeds are highly intelligent and can quickly be trained. Another feature shared by most toy dogs is that they are attractive and neat-looking little animals.

The toy group has representatives drawn from many other breed types, as well as some which are unique to the group. The terriers are represented in the shape of the Australian Silky Terrier, the Yorkshire Terrier, and the

Although toy dogs are small and easy for children to handle, they should still be afforded the same respect as a larger breed.

Miniature Pinscher. These dogs, although small, have typical terrier characteristics of bravery and dash.

For admirers of spaniels the choice in the toy dog group includes the Pekingese, the King Charles Spaniel, and the Cavalier King Charles Spaniel. Lovers of spitz-type dogs will find the Pomeranian has all the spark and energy – and the voice – of its larger cousins.

Exotic, long-coated dogs come no better than in the form of the Papillon, the Pekingese, and the Yorkshire Terrier, and for grace and elegance it would be hard to find a better example than the Italian Greyhound – truly a Greyhound in miniature. And for sheer character and a look of pure mischief nothing can beat the Brussels Griffon.

The Miniature Pinscher has the bravery of its larger cousin.

OPPOSITE: The Pomeranian is a Spitz-type breed.

AUSTRALIAN SILKY TERRIER

This breed came about in the 1800s as the result of crossings between the Yorkshire Terrier and the Australian Terrier. It was formerly known as the Sydney Silky Terrier, after a well-known breeder of these dogs moved to the city of that name with his kennels.

A low-slung, long-coated dog with a refined look about it, the head is wedge-shaped, with a moderately-broad, flat skull. The nose is black. The eyes are round, small, and have an alert expression. The ears are V-shaped and pricked. The neck is slightly arched and is carried on a longish body. The legs are short and finely-boned. The tail is usually docked and carried erect.

The coat is fine, straight, long, and glossy with a silky texture. Colors are blue-and-tan, and gray-blue-and-tan.

The long, fine coat and generally elegant appearance of this breed should not disguise the fact that the Silky is a real terrier! Keen, active and ever-ready, this dog makes a friendly companion with plenty of stamina.

Size *Height:* 9in (23cm). *Weight:* 9lb (4kg).

BRUSSELS GRIFFON

This dog originated in Belgium, where it was used in stables for keeping down vermin and for raising the alarm on approaching strangers. Dogs very similar to the Brussels Griffon were depicted in paintings in the 1400s, and the breed was well-established by the 1600s. Two varieties exist – a rough-coated form and a smooth-coated form known as the Petit Brabançon.

A square, well-built little dog with a monkey-like face, the head has a broad, round skull, a short, wide muzzle, and a prominent chin. The nose is black. The eyes are large and round. The ears are semi-erect. The medium-length neck is slightly arched, and the deep-chested body is carried on

As the name suggests, the Brussels Griffon originated in Belgium, taking its name from the City of Brussels.

straight, medium-length legs. The tail is usually docked.

The coat can be in two distinctive types; *Rough-coated:* Hard and wiry, but not curly; prominent walrus moustache. *Smooth-coated:* Short and tight. Colors are red, beige, black-and tan, or black.

No other dog has such a mischievous face, and this is especially apparent in the rough-coated variety. Lively, fearless, and alert, the Brussels Griffon makes a happy and amusing pet dog for owners living in town or country.

Size *Height:* 7–8in (18–20.5cm).
Weight: 5–11lb (2.5–5kg).

CAVALIER KING CHARLES SPANIEL

This breed has been known for several centuries, and was a popular dog in European courts in the 17th century. Larger than its relative the King Charles Spaniel, and with less of a snub nose, the Cavalier King Charles Spaniel achieved Kennel Club recognition in the 1940s.

An attractive, well-balanced small spaniel, the head has a flattish skull and a short, square muzzle. The nose is black. The large, round eyes are dark in color and have a trusting, endearing expression. The ears are long and pendulous, with good feathering. The neck is of medium length and slightly arched. The body is short with a level back and is carried on moderately-boned legs. The tail is fairly long, although sometimes it is docked by one-third.

The coat is long and silky, sometimes with a slight wave; ample feathering. Colors are black-and-tan, ruby (rich red), Blenheim (chestnut-and-white), or tricolor (black, white and tan).

One of the most popular of all the toy breeds, the Cavalier King Charles Spaniel seems to offer everything in that it is friendly, as happy to run in the fields as it is to sit by its owner's side. Despite its diminutive size it is built like a proper sporting dog and is easy to feed and groom.

Size *Height:* 13in (33cm).
Weight: 12 18lb (5.5–8kg).

The Cavalier King Charles is the ideal companion. Playful and cheerful, it loves to run around. It is equally happly to sit by its owner's side.

CHIHUAHUA

This dog gets its name from the Mexican state of Chihuahua where, around the mid-1890s, it first became well-known to the Western world – although there is evidence that it may have actually originated in the Orient. Soon after, the dog was introduced into the United States, where the breed standard was improved. The Chihuahua comes in two varieties – a smooth-coated and a long-coated form. This is generally considered to be the world's smallest breed of dog.

A tiny, neat-looking dog with a prominent head. The head has a broad, rounded skull, and a short, pointed muzzle and a distinct stop. The large, round eyes are set well apart; several colors are possible,

The Chihuahua, despite its small stature, has a large spirit and brave heart.

according to coat color. The distinctive ears are large and flared and set at the side of the head. The slightly-arched neck is carried on an elongated body with a level back. The legs are moderately well-boned and of medium length. The tail is carried over the back.

The coat can be in two distinctive types; *Smooth-coated:* Smooth, soft, and glossy. *Long-coated:* Soft, and flat or wavy; feathering on feet, legs, and ruff. Any colors are permissible.

Despite its diminutive size, the Chihuahua is a spirited and intelligent dog that moves with a swift and purposeful action. It is friendly but will raise the alarm at the approach of unknown visitors to the house.

Size *Height:* 6–9in (15–23cm).
Weight: 2–6lb (1–3kg).

"Heaven goes by favor. If it went by merit, you would stay out and your dog would go in."

Mark Twain (1835–1910)

CHINESE CRESTED DOG

A favorite dog of the Han Dynasty in ancient China, the Chinese Crested was used to guard treasures and even in some forms of hunting. The dog was first shown in America in 1885. The breed comes in two coat forms: the hairless (with a crest of hair on the head, hair covering parts of the legs and feet and a plume of hair on the tail) and the powder puff (with a body covered in fine hair).

An active and graceful dog, the head has a moderately-broad, elongated skull and a medium-long, tapering muzzle. The nose may be any color. The almond-shaped eyes are almost black and are set wide apart. The large ears are held erect in the hairless variety, but drop ears are permitted in the powder puff type. The neck is long and lean. The body is of medium length with a deep chest. The legs are long and lightly-boned and end in hare-feet. The tail is long and tapering.

The coat comes in two forms; *Hairless:* Hair confined to head crest, lower legs and feet and tail plume; the skin may be plain or spotted and may lighten in summer. *Powder puff:* Coat consists of a soft veil of long hair. Any colors are allowed.

Happy, lively, and affectionate, the Chinese Crested Dog is a tough breed that keeps itself very clean. The dog enjoys reasonable amounts of exercise. The hairless variety, in particular, can easily become sunburnt.

Size *Height:* dog 11–13in (28–33cm); bitch 9–12in (23–30.5cm). *Weight:* 12lb (5.5kg).

OPPOSITE: A Powder Puff Chinese Crested Dog.

Hairless Chinese Crested puppies.

HAVANESE

Known as the national dog of Cuba, the Havanese was probably brought to the country by traders or Spanish colonists. Many of these dogs were subsequently taken to the United States when their owners fled the Cuban communist revolution. The dog is also known as the Bichon Havanais.

A long-coated, well-built, bichon-type dog, the head has a broad skull, a pointed muzzle, and a moderate stop. The nose is usually black, but may be brown in some coat shades. The large, almond-shaped eyes are dark and have a kindly expression. The drop ears are moderately pointed. The neck is of medium length, and the body has a level topline with a slight rise over the loins. The legs are fairly short and medium-boned and end in hare-feet. The tail, usually carried high over the back, is covered in long, silky hair.

The coat is soft and silky, with a dense crest on the head. Any color is allowed, such as white, cream, black, blue, chocolate, or silver.

Friendly, lively and intelligent, the Havanese is a tough little character that can stand up for itself in most situations but fits well into family life.

Size *Height:* 8–11in (20.5–28cm). *Weight:* 7–12lb (3–5.5kg).

ITALIAN GREYHOUND

Dogs very similar in appearance to this breed can be seen depicted in the tombs of ancient pharaohs, although the modern Italian Greyhound was probably bred more recently in Roman times. This is the smallest of the sighthounds, and its diminutive size precludes serious chasing as part of a hunt. Instead, it is admired for its small-scale elegance, ease of keeping and gentle nature.

A Greyhound in miniature, the head has a long, flat, narrow skull, and a fine, long muzzle. The nose may be any dark color. The eyes are expressive, large and bright. The delicate, rose-shaped ears are set well back on the head. The long neck is gracefully arched and is carried on a narrow, deep-chested body; the back is slightly arched over the loins. The legs are long and well-muscled and end in hare-feet. The tail is long and fine and carried low.

The coat is satin-like, fine and short. Colors are black, blue, cream, fawn, red, white – or any of the colors with white.

Despite its fragile appearance, the Italian Greyhound is brave and energetic. It has a good turn of speed over the countryside, moving with the same long-striding gait as its larger cousins. The dog is also affectionate, and perfectly happy to sit at home next to its owner.

Size *Height:* 13–15in (33–38cm).
Weight: 6–10lb (3–4.5kg).

The Italian Greyhound is quiet and gentle and would perhaps feel happier in a home that has no young children. It is a perfect miniature of its larger cousin.

MALTESE

The Maltese, or Maltese Terrier, is one of the oldest breeds in Europe. It was probably introduced to Malta by Phoenician traders sailing around the Mediterranean, and there is evidence of the dog being admired by early civilizations such as the Ancient Greeks. The Romans also kept these small dogs as pets, and they were popular again in the Middle Ages.

A neat little dog with a profuse white coat, the head has a flat skull and a short, broad muzzle. The nose is black. The eyes are dark-brown and have an intelligent expression. The ears are long, well-feathered, and pendulous. The body is short and cobby and carried on short, straight legs. The tail, also well-feathered, is carried arched over the back.

The coat is long, straight, and silky. The color should be pure white, although occasional lemon markings may appear.

The Maltese moves with a free-flowing action, seeming to glide along with the coat wafting around it. Although small, this is a tough, friendly and alert dog that likes to play and enjoys exercise. The coat needs plenty of grooming to keep it in peak condition.

Size *Height:* 10in (25.5cm). *Weight:* 4–6lb (2–3kg).

MINIATURE PINSCHER

A German breed, the Miniature Pinscher is – as its name suggests – the smallest of the pinschers. The Miniature Pinscher was bred from German terriers about 100 years ago and is now widely popular.

A compact, elegant, smooth-coated small dog, the head is long with a flat skull and a strong muzzle. The nose is usually black, but in blue- or chocolate-coated dogs it may harmonize with the coat color. The eyes are usually black. The ears may be carried erect or in the half-dropped position. The neck is graceful and arched and carried on a short, moderately deep-chested body. The legs are

The dainty Miniature Pinscher, despite being small in stature, is brave and alert. They make good watchdogs as they are naturally wary of strangers.

straight and medium-boned. The tail may be docked short or left natural –
if the latter, it is often carried arched over the body.

The coat is smooth, straight, hard, and glossy.
Colors are black, blue, chocolate with tan markings,
or various shades of red.

Small it may be, but the Miniature Pinscher is a
fearless, active and alert dog, moving with a characteristic,
high-stepping gait. It also has an excellent sense of hearing
and will bark to alert the household if
strangers approach.

Size *Height:* 10–12in (25.5–30.5cm).
Weight: 7.5lb (3.5kg).

"A dog is the only thing on earth
that loves you more than he
loves himself."
Josh Billings (1818–1885)

PAPILLON

The Papillon, also known as the Butterfly Dog because of the shape of its ears, is recognized as a Franco-Belgian breed. In fact, there are two versions of this dog – one with erect ears (the origin of the name 'Papillon') and the other with drop ears. Once popular in the royal courts of Europe, the dog is still much admired today.

An alert, silky-coated dog, the head has a slightly rounded skull and a pointed muzzle with a well-defined stop. The nose is black. The medium-sized eyes are dark and alert. The ears are of two types: either erect and held like the open wings of a butterfly, or carried dropped; in either style the ears are well-fringed with hair. The body is long, with a level back, and is carried on finely-boned legs that end in hare-feet. The long tail is arched over the back and falls to one side.

The coat is full, flowing, long, and silky; the chest has a profuse frill. The coat is white with patches of any color except liver; the preferred markings on the head include a white stripe down the center of the skull that helps to accentuate the butterfly effect.

Intelligent, affectionate, and easy to train, the attractive little Papillon proves itself a star performer in obedience tests. The dog is a delightful companion, but is not recommended as a pet for small children.

Size *Height:* 8–11in (20.5–28cm).
Weight: 7.5lb (3.5kg).

The charming Papillon remains the heart-stealer it was when it was a member of the French Court. Today, it is still loved for its playfulness and strong sense of fun.

PEKINGESE

Once the sacred dog of China, and named after the capital city of that country, this little dog is another of those breeds that is recognized by people the world over. Its ancestry can be traced back to at least the 8th century Tang Dynasty, and for centuries the Pekingese was highly prized at the Imperial Court. Perhaps this royal patronage explains something of the sense of self-importance which the Pekingese seems to convey. In the 1860s, some examples of the breed were brought to England after Peking was overrun, and in the early 1900s it was introduced to America.

A small, well-balanced, and long-coated dog with a characteristic monkey face. The head is large, with a broad skull and a short, broad, wrinkled muzzle with a strong under

244

jaw. The flat nose is black. The eyes are large and round. The ears are heart-shaped and pendulous. The short neck is carried on a short body with a broad chest. The short legs are well-boned, the hind legs being lighter. The well-feathered tail is carried curled tightly over one side of the back.

The coat is long and thick with a full mane and good feathering on the ears, legs, tail and feet; the outercoat is coarse and there is a thick undercoat. All colors are allowed except liver or albino.

Playful and fearless, the Pekingese is also an affectionate dog that makes a highly individual pet. But this is not a breed that takes kindly to long walks in the country, preferring to amble along at its own speed with a characteristic rolling gait. The coat needs plenty of regular grooming to keep it looking its best.

Size *Height:* 7in (18cm). *Weight:* dog 11lb (5kg); bitch 12lb (5.5kg).

The Pekingese is not the most active of dogs and is content to amble along at its own pace. It does, however, require regular grooming to maintain its coat in good condition.

245

POMERANIAN

This is the smallest of the spitz-type dogs and is a descendant of the big sled-pulling dogs of the Arctic region. This German dog came to Britain in the late 1870s, and its popularity later received a boost when Queen Victoria decide to keep the breed.

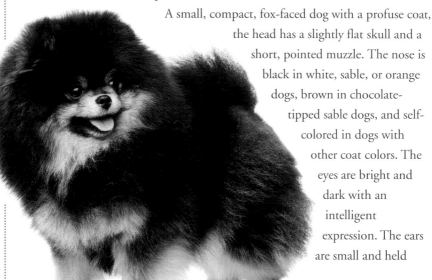

A small, compact, fox-faced dog with a profuse coat, the head has a slightly flat skull and a short, pointed muzzle. The nose is black in white, sable, or orange dogs, brown in chocolate-tipped sable dogs, and self-colored in dogs with other coat colors. The eyes are bright and dark with an intelligent expression. The ears are small and held erect. The body is short, with a deep chest, and is carried on finely-boned, medium-length legs. The tail is carried over the back in typical spitz fashion.

The outercoat is long, straight, and harsh, and very thick around the neck and shoulders; undercoat is soft and thick. All colors are permitted, such as white, black, cream, brown, orange, beaver, or sable.

Pomeranians have plenty of energy, just like their larger cousins. Extroverted and vivacious, the dog makes a lively companion. It also has a shrill bark to alert its owner when strangers approach the house.

Size *Height:* 8.5–11in (21.5–28cm).
Weight: dog 4–4.5lb (1.8–2kg);
bitch 4.5–5.5lb (2–2.5kg).

The Pomeranian makes a lively little companion. Like all Spitz-type breeds it has a good deal of energy. Despite its size it is also a very good watchdog.

PUG

The Pug is thought to have originated in China, where the dog was the companion of monks. It arrived in Europe with traders in the 1500s and subsequently became very popular in the Netherlands and in Britain.

A square, muscular dog reminiscent of a miniature mastiff. The head is large and round with a short, blunt muzzle; the skin has clearly-defined wrinkles. The huge, dark eyes are set in their sockets in a way that makes them seem globular; they are also highly expressive. The ears are small and thin, and there are two types – drop rose ears or folded button ears; the latter are preferred. The neck is strong

The Pug is a muscular little dog, rather like a miniature mastiff. It may look tough but it is actually quite a softee – gentle and loving.

and thick and is carried on a short, wide-chested body. The fairly long legs are strong and straight. The tail is held curled tightly over the hip.

The coat is short, smooth, soft, and glossy. Colors are silver, fawn, apricot, or black; light colors should have clearly contrasting markings including a dark mask and ears.

The sturdy Pug is a real character among dogs. The body language and the almost talking eyes can express all manner of moods from alert watchfulness to an appealing request for attention.

Size *Height:* 10–11in (25.5–28cm).
Weight: 14–18lb (6.5–8kg).

"The dog is the most faithful of animals and would be much esteemed were it not so common. Our Lord God has made His greatest gifts the commonest."
Martin Luther (1483–1546)

SHIH TZU

The Shih Tzu comes originally from Tibet, although it was developed in China and found favor in the royal courts of the imperial palaces. Records dating back to 624 AD show dogs very similar to the Shih Tzu being given as tributes to the Tang Emperor. The name Shih Tzu translates as 'lion dog,' and is believed to be a reference to the dog's brave character rather than to its appearance. The first examples of this breed to be seen in Britain occurred in 1931.

A long-coated little dog with a very proud carriage, the head is broad and round with a short, square muzzle. The nose is usually black but may be liver-colored in liver or liver-marked dogs. The eyes are large, round, and dark and have a friendly expression. The ears are large and pendulous. The body is long with a deep chest. The legs are short, muscular, and well-boned. The well-plumed tail is carried curled over the back.

The Shih Tzu has a long, straight coat, with a dense undercoat; a slight wave is permitted in the coat, but not a curl; the hair should form a good beard and whiskers, and hair growing upwards over the nose bridge should create the familiar 'chrysanthemum' look. All colors are allowed.

An outgoing, enthusiastic little dog, the Shih Tzu is also intelligent and friendly and makes a good family addition. Moderate exercise is all that the dog requires, but regular grooming is needed to keep the coat glossy and tangle-free.

Size *Height:* dog 10.5in (27cm); bitch 9in (23cm). *Weight:* 10–16lb (4.5–7kg).

The Shih Tzu is a confident and dignified little dog. However, it still loves to play and has a fun-loving nature.

YORKSHIRE TERRIER

The result of crossings involving the Black-and-Tan Terrier, the Skye Terrier, the Dandie Dinmont and the Maltese, the 'Yorkie' first came to prominence in the 1850s. Originally the Yorkshire Terrier was bred as a rat-fighting dog; then, the breed was larger than the show and pet dogs seen today.

A compact, long-coated small terrier, the head is quite small with a flattish skull and a short muzzle. The nose is black. The dark eyes are medium-sized and have an intelligent, alert expression. The small V-shaped ears are carried erect. The compact body has a level back and is

The Yorkshire Terrier is a true terrier at heart, having been bred to fight rats. It is always alert and ready for action.

carried on shortish, straight legs. The tail is usually docked to about half its natural length.

The coat is long and straight and glossy with a silky texture; hair longer on the head. The main body color is dark steel-blue, with the hair on the head a rich golden-tan, and the hair on the chest a bright tan color.

Groomed to the peak of perfection for the show ring, it is hard to believe that this dog, with its lustrous, flowing coat, and colorful bows in its hair, is also, given half the chance, a typical terrier.

Size *Height:* dog 8in (20.5cm); bitch 7in (18cm).
Weight: 7lb (3kg).

"My little dog; a heartbeat at my feet."
Edith Wharton (1862–1937)